Routledge Revivals

System, Structure and Experience

First Published in 1970, *System, Structure and Experience* offers a basic information-flow design capable of accounting for the complex operations of a culturally cognizant and purposive mind consistent with the general relationship of the human organism and its environment. By means of the isomorphy of a hierarchically ordered series of circuits, a way is opened for resolving the traditional 'mind- body' or 'psycho-physical' problems. The work outlines the design of a self-stabilizing and self-organizing system, shows that it applies to artificial, biological as well as cognitive structures, and then undertakes to analyze the diverse facets of perpetual, scientific, aesthetic, and religious experience in its terms. The interrelation of the two or more such multi-level cognitive systems offers insights into the problems of human communication.

The book is a contribution to the scientific analysis of cognitive experience and promotes the transfer of the traditional domain of an introspectively founded philosophy of mind into the realm of modern system research.

System, Structure and Experience
Toward a Scientific Theory of Mind

Ervin Laszlo

First published in 1970
by Gordon & Breach Science Publishers, Inc.

This edition first published in 2024 by Routledge
4 Park Square, Milton Park, Abingdon, Oxon, OX14 4RN

and by Routledge
605 Third Avenue, New York, NY 10017

Routledge is an imprint of the Taylor & Francis Group, an informa business

© 1969 by Gordon & Breach Science Publishers, Inc.

All rights reserved. No part of this book may be reprinted or reproduced or utilised in any form or by any electronic, mechanical, or other means, now known or hereafter invented, including photocopying and recording, or in any information storage or retrieval system, without permission in writing from the publishers.

Publisher's Note
The publisher has gone to great lengths to ensure the quality of this reprint but points out that some imperfections in the original copies may be apparent.

Disclaimer
The publisher has made every effort to trace copyright holders and welcomes correspondence from those they have been unable to contact.

A Library of Congress record exists under LCCN: 76092091

ISBN: 978-1-032-83091-9 (hbk)
ISBN: 978-1-003-50772-7 (ebk)
ISBN: 978-1-032-83092-6 (pbk)

Book DOI 10.4324/9781003507727

System, Structure, and Experience

Toward a Scientific Theory of Mind

ERVIN LASZLO

UNITED NATIONS INSTITUTE
FOR TRAINING AND RESEARCH
(UNITAR)

GORDON AND BREACH SCIENCE PUBLISHERS
New York   London   Paris

Copyright © 1969 by Gordon and Breach, Science Publishers, Inc.

Gordon and Breach, Science Publishers, Inc.
One Park Avenue
New York, New York 10016

Gordon and Breach Science Publishers Ltd.
42 William IV Street
London WC2N 4DF

Gordon & Breach
7-9 rue Emile Dubois
75014 Paris

First Published February 1970
Second Printing February 1978

Library of Congress catalog card number 76-92091. ISBN 0 677 02360 X. All rights reserved. No part of this book may be reproduced or utilized in any form or by any means, electronic or mechanical, including photocopying, recording, or by any information storage and retrieval system, without permission in writing from the publishers.

Printed in the United States of America.

*For Professor F. S. C. Northrop,
in sincere friendship and admiration*

Preface

The true method of philosophy, Whitehead said in his Preface to *Process and Reality*, is to frame a scheme of ideas, the best that one can, and unflinchingly to explore the interpretation of experience in terms of that scheme. The present work offers such an 'unflinching interpretation' of experience, in terms of a scheme of ideas based on concepts recently developed in the new scientific disciplines of cybernetics, information theory systems-analysis and general system theory. It lies therefore in an interdisciplinary area, and is addressed as much to the scientific as to the philosophic community.

The above mentioned new disciplines offer means for attacking traditional philosophical problems with fresh and testable concepts. They encourage hopes that some problems, in the past associated with philosophy, may pass in the future to the realm of science. The passage will probably involve an intermediate stage where the concepts and theories developed in special sciences are applied to problems belonging to the sphere of speculative philosophy. The works in that stage will be proto-scientific working hypotheses, to be tested for applicability and refined to higher levels of accuracy. The present work comes into that category. It is not purely 'speculative philosophy' and not yet 'science.' It may be considered, if the reader so wishes, 'scientific philosophy' or 'philosophical science.' But it may be that these labels are overly optimistic. Prior to the systematic criticism which its publication can bring about, its author would prefer to consider it a working hypothesis, contributing, if successful, to the annexation of a field—the sphere of human experience and the phenomenon of mind—by science. Such transfer will not empoverish philosophy, for there is no dearth of philosophical problems, many of which are generated by science itself—but will enrich science. This passage, to be envisaged for the next few decades, is in accord with a general tendency originated since the 1950s. Since then, perhaps more than ever before, the work traditionally performed by speculative philosophers is being taken over by scientists operating on new 'hybrid' fields. In virtue of this trend, new and improved techniques and conceptual frameworks are offered for explaining a wide range of phenomena in consistent and testable general theories. Concern shifts from ultra-specialization and analysis of detached facts, to the development of general principles, applicable beyond the genus of facts in view of which they were initially postulated. To the extent of the success of this much needed trend, science becomes philosophical and philosophy becomes scientific. There is a meeting of interests, an agreement on basic concerns.

The present work, the outcome of some years of thought, and bearing the scars as well as the fruits of reformulations effected after numerous expositions in public lectures, is dedicated to furthering this trend. It may have something of value to offer, or it may be misguided. But, in the words of Whitehead, a great precursor of the present trend, a new idea introduces a new alternative; and we are no less indebted to the thinker when we adopt the alternative which he discarded. In this perspective, the author believes that his work has a contribution to make to the reader's own thinking on the problems. And the problems, at all events, are of the first magnitude, well deserving of all the sustained thought we can muster.

Spring, 1969

Acknowledgements

It is the author's pleasant duty to record his sincere thanks to several distinguished colleagues who have read his manuscript, at various stages of its completion. In particular, he has greatly profited from the detailed comments of Professors Stephen C. Pepper, Henry Margenau, Alastair Taylor, Donald H. Andrews, William Edgar, James B. Wilbur and Rubin Gotesky. He would also like to thank Professor Lee Thayer for permission to reprint part of the author's "Multilevel Feedback Theory of Mind" from *Communication: General Semantics Prospectives* (Spartan Books: New York, 1969), as part of Chapter 1.

Contents

	Preface	vii
1	Basic Information-flow Design for Self-stabilizing Self-organizing Systems	1
2	The System-theoretical Analysis of Experience	16
3	Levels of Controlled Information-flow in Experience	29
4	Multilevel Interpersonal Communication	78
5	Values in Cognitive Communication	93
6	Conclusions	98
	Appendix—Further Notes on the Perception of Invariant Intelligible *Gestalten*	101
	Index	109

CHAPTER I

Basic Information-flow Design for Self-stabilizing Self-organizing Systems*

Can we account for the manifest facts of our experience without either unverifiable *ad hoc* principles or reducing them to chemistry and physics? Nondulist and nonreductionist frameworks belonged traditionally to the domain of metaphysics. Today, such frameworks may be in the offing within the sciences. The importance of modern structuralist and system-analytical research lies in the fact that they offer new conceptual frameworks for the nonreductionist unification of phenomena in diverse fields of investigation. They employ uniform conceptual constructs and encourage the belief that the unified framework of their explanation implies a unity of the objects of explanation. Systems on the electromechanical, electronic, chemical, biological, psychological and even sociological sectors of inquiry can be nonreductively treated in reference to invariant constructs which include the notions of totality, transformation, invariance, system, noise, message, information-flow, feedback, multivariable interaction, and so on. It should be possible to explore the interpretation of the higher cognitive reaches of the mind and experience in reference to the unitary system-theoretical framework. The unknown variables are too numerous in that sphere of inquiry to permit the exploration to lay claim to scientific rigor. But it should be possible to hypothetically survey the phenomenon of mind and the realm of human experience in reference to concepts developed by cyberneticians and information and system theoreticians. The consideration, that herewith a major philosophical problem—the 'mind-body' or, 'psycho-physical' problem—is being attacked from an integrative yet non-reductionist angle, should offset the intrinsic uncertainties. On this domain we must, for the time being, content ourselves with offering the 'likeliest tale' but, since not all tales are equally likely, our task becomes, nevertheless

* The reader more interested in philosophy than system theory may skip this chapter and refer back to it subsequently, if in need of elucidation.

an exacting one. This work is offered in the belief that the next decades will adduce important evidence to the effect that the *likeliest* 'tale of mind and human experience is a structuralist and system-theoretical one.

Let me set about, now, the task of constructing a model for the *simplest possible system* which could perform the operations observed of the human mind.[1] I shall proceed on the assumption, made already by the Milesian natural philosophers of the 6th century B.C., that the 'buzzing confusion' of the senses is ordered into items of invariant knowledge by our minds. Whatever else the mind may perform, it does stand out with some degree of finality, that it performs the feat of extracting ordered 'message' from chaotic 'noise.' It may, perhaps, be possible to conceive of complex mental functions as specific qualifications and special cases of the mind's fundamental invariance-extracting capacity. I shall assume that this hypothesis is worthy of being followed up and shall proceed forthwith to propose an optimally simple scheme of information-flow capable of reducing a variable fluctuating noise-source to elements of ordered invariance.

I postulate an information-flow between a variable noise source (E), an input (P), an output (R) and a control-coding (or coupling) between input and output (C). Let the information-flow be undirectional proceeding as $E \rightarrow P \rightarrow C \rightarrow R \rightarrow E$ ... in a continuous circuit. E provides the noise which is potentially reducible to invariant messages (fig. 1). P acts as a filter, admitting some elements of the noise provided by E and excluding others. The admitted elements are conduced to R via C. That is, the system's output depends not merely on the filtered information transmitted by P, but on the relevance of that information to C. Input and output are coupled by the coding in C, with the result that R occurs as a specifically

(1)

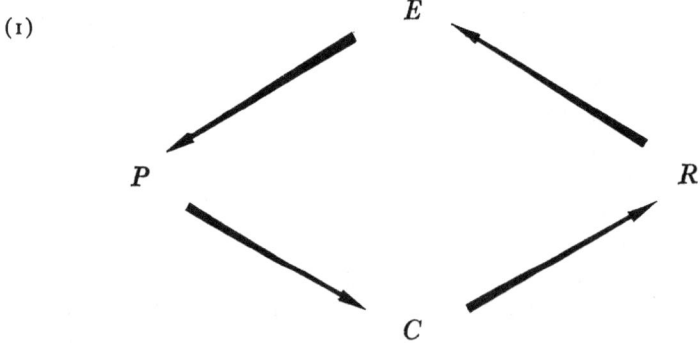

---

[1] It will be evident that I am using the deductive, rather than the inductive method. The use and success of this method is such, that employing it requires no particular justification.

coordinated response of the relevance of P to C. From R, the flow of information takes us back to E and thus back again through the other elements of the circuit. So far, then, we have an ongoing flow of information between four components: E, P, C, R.

Figure (1), as all those which will follow it, suffers from the deficiency of two-dimensional representation. Due to the temporal extension of the information-flow, it should be represented by an ascending helix:

(2)

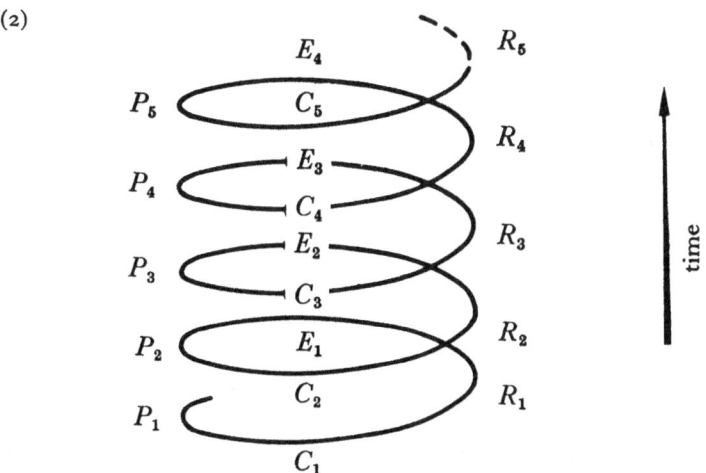

But for the sake of simplicity and better visual maneuverability, I shall continue to use figure (1) rather than figure (2). Now, although by means of this circuit the noise is filtered and specific qualifying responses are injected into it, no provision has been made for the deciphering of the 'message.' The latter emerges if the condition of invariance of C with respect to P is observed. Specifically, I shall consider as ordered information an input which satisfies C as the transformation of an invariance. The invariance which C incorporates is a certain pattern in P. If that pattern is produced, C leads to the specifically coordinated output. The code represents a factor of invariance which extends over a permissible range of transformations. If P falls within this range, it satisfies the code and response is correspondingly produced. Therefore, the message for the system consists in the matching of C by P. Such a 'matched flow' corresponds to the intrinsic standard of the system and, I shall say, represents 'intelligibility' for it. The system can produce its coordinated responses whenever P filters information from E which matches C. This eventuality is represented in figure (3).

The double-shafted arrow signifies that P is a transformation of C.

4   *System, Structure, and Experience*

But, unless we provide for goal-directedness in the system, the occurrence of this matched flow is merely a matter of chance. It depends on E providing such noise which, when filtered through P, happens to coincide with

(3)
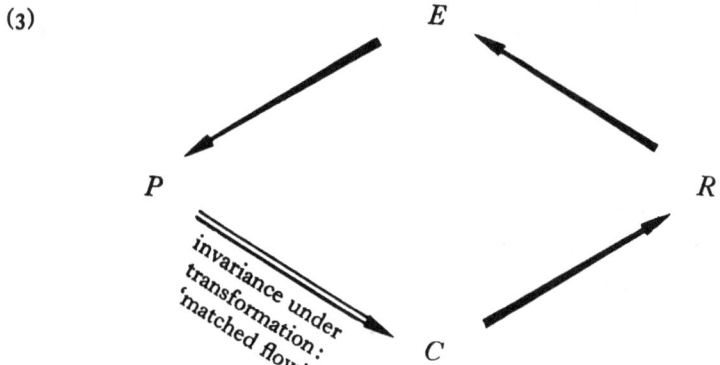

the code C. The system can make provisions for the greater probability of this occurrence, however. Let us not forget that R is a specific response to a given instance of invariance under transformation in the input and in its coding. R, then, can be conceived as a response to this state, which is directed at E, the source of all potential information, in function of producing therein a noise-source which, when filtered, matches the system's intrinsic code. That is, the output conditions the input to maximize the chances of the input satisfying the code on the basis of which the output was produced. By this token the code is self-stabilizing: it gives rise to an output which increases the probability of an input which matches it. Thus we get:

(4)
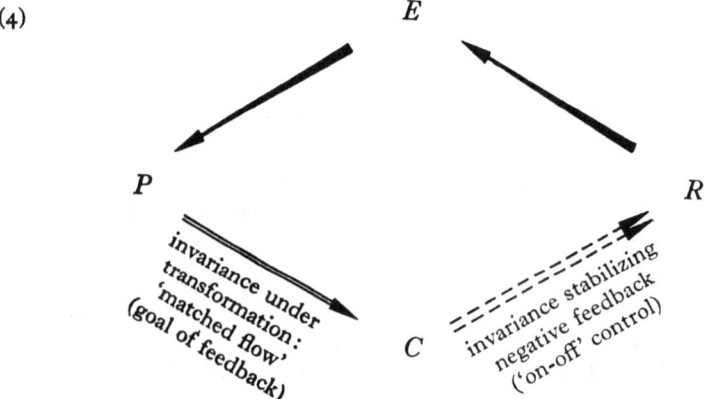

Here we have the concept of negative feedback illustrated in our scheme.

Basic Information-flow Design for Self-stabilizing Self-organizing Systems

It is one which presupposes an ongoing flow of information between the components, controlled by an incorporated code or standard which tends to perpetuate itself. The result is that E becomes progressively ordered. It becomes more and more conformant to the requirement that, when it is filtered by P, the information left over should be a 'message' which satisfies the code.

And now I shall complete the axiomatic construction by adding another feature to the system, a most remarkable one: adaptation. I propose that the code is not fixed but adaptable to the information transmitted by P. That is, the system is not only self-stabilizing, but *self-organizing*. It adjusts its codes to the type of input it tends to receive. It possesses the remarkable property of searching out factors of invariance within the range of its actual input. We can conceive of this as follows. Inadequate information-content in P leads to exploratory responses, rather than occasioning the absence of response. The system is such that a given code perpetuates itself through the response only if it is matched by the input. Otherwise it is replaced by alternate codes which, through R and E, affect the input. If any code produces a response which results in a matching input, it is perpetuated. Full coincidence between input and code issues in the establishment of the successful code in place of the previous unsuccessful one. The self-organizing adaptation of the system to its noise-source may be represented thus:

5)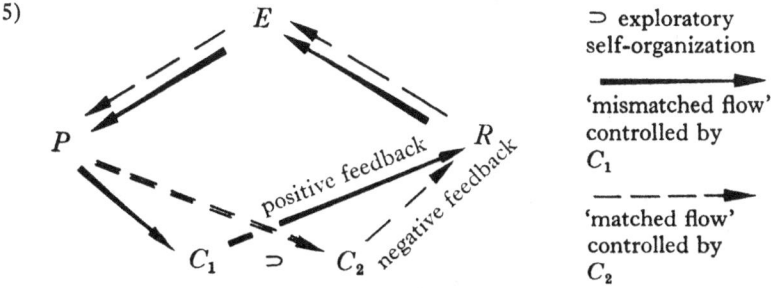

The adaptive self-organization of the system is a precondition of its functioning if E is subject to change. As a result of changes in E, a code which functioned adequately at one time may cease so to function at another time. When that happens, the adaptive function is called into play: positive feedback explorations locate new codes and the negative feedback system stabilizes its flow until further changes in E produce a mismatch of input and code, calling for renewed adaptive self-organization. Thus the system continually maps its changing environment in its codes.

The outcome of the self-stabilizing and self-organizing functions of the system is a continually maintained correlation between the codes of the system and its environment. The correlation is brought about manipulatively in the self-stabilizing system: such a system can be said to 'project' its code into the environment:

(6)
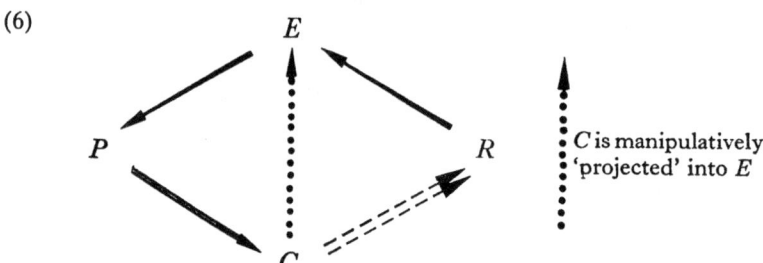
C is manipulatively 'projected' into E

The same correlation between the state of the environment and the codes of the system is effected adaptively by the self-organizing system: this system 'maps' the state of the environment in its codes:

(7)
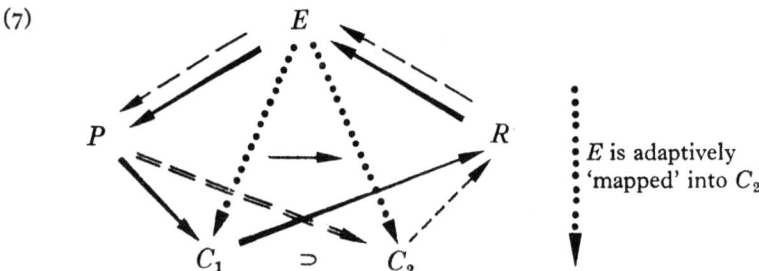
E is adaptively 'mapped' into C_2

Thus the functioning of self-stabilizing and self-organizing systems brings about the continual correlation of their codes and environment, signalled through the match of input and code (i.e. by the code being invariant in regard to the input). Such functioning may appear to be teleological in character but has nothing intrinsically qualitative and mysterious about it: goal-directedness can now be defined in rigorous mathematical terms, as properties of physical (or other) systems, following Somerhoff's concept of 'directive correlation'[1] and Wiener's concept of feedback control. Rather than assuming that the self-stabilizing and self-organizing system is guided by some anticipated final cause or entelechy, we can hold that the components of the system are directively correlated to achieve the goals over a given range of conditions, and that the mechanism of this goal-directedness is positive and negative feedback.

[1] Cf. G. Somerhoff, *Analytical Biology* (Oxford, 1950), and pp. 12ff below.

Basic Information-flow Design for Self-stabilizing Self-organizing Systems

The above is, this writer believes, the simplest possible information-flow model of the human mind. It is the model of a system which both manipulatively and adaptively derives message from noise and thereby maintains a running representation of its environment as well as maintaining an environment suited to its representations. The importance of the model is, first, that it applies *in principle* to any control system of the corresponding properties, regardless of the specific nature of the components and materials; second, that it applies *in fact* to biological systems (organisms); and third, that it applies—as I shall show in detail—to the structure and flow of information in human experience. Each of these contentions will be considered in turn.

I

To devise an artificial regulatory system specifically designed to satisfy the foregoing scheme would be time consuming and, so far at least, unfeasible in practice. Instead, I can refer to a well-known scheme which satisfies my postulates in all major respects, regardless of whether or not an artificial system could actually be built on its basis. I am referring to MacKay's information-flow model of human behavior.[1]

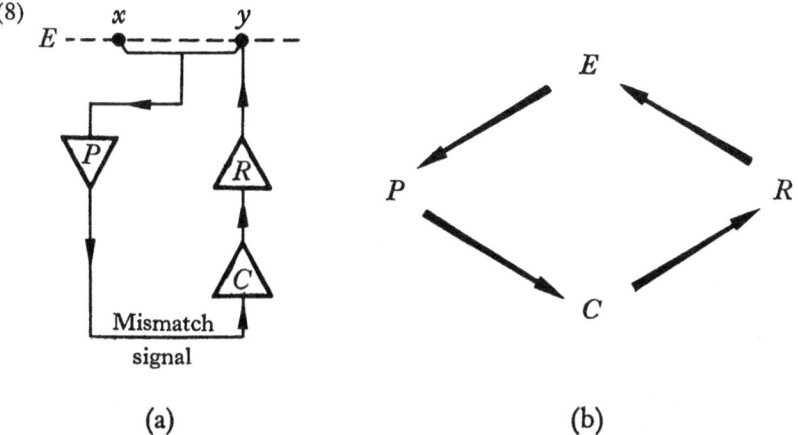

(a)   (b)

MacKay develops a theoretic design for a goal-guided artificial system having system-components which he identifies as *receptor, control, effector* and *field*. The flow of information proceeds from the field, through the receptor, to control, and effector, and back to the field. By using my

[1] Donald M. MacKay, 'Towards an Information-Flow Model of Human Behaviour,' *British Journal of Psychology*, 47 (1956).

symbols in MacKay's scheme[1] and placing it next to figure (1), the basic logic of relations in the information-flow appears isomorphic (fig. 8).

In MacKay's system, the behavior of the effector (R) is controlled by information received from the field (E) through the receptors (P). The information is in the form of a 'mismatch signal' if the programed 'goal' of the system and its actual state do not coincide (e.g. in figure (8), where the goal is point X on the field E and the actual state of the system corresponds to point Y). In the event that the goal has been reached, the mismatch signal is replaced by a 'match' signal. One can extrapolate this state of the system and represent the match signal consistently with my own notation, by a double-shafted arrow:

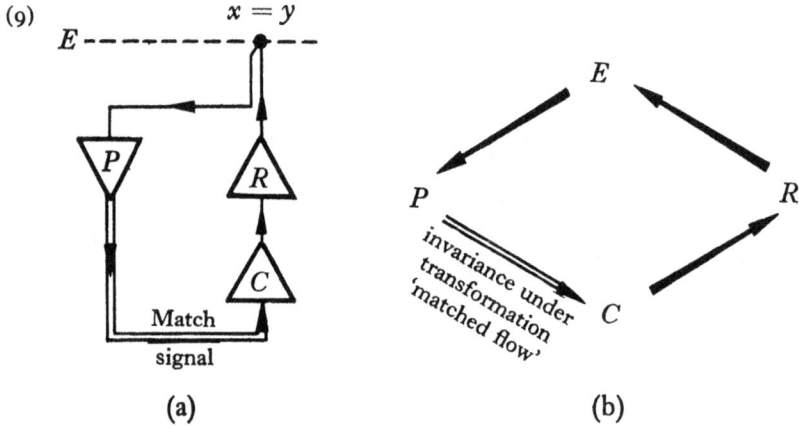

(9)

(a)   (b)

The structure of the information-flow remains isomorphic to figure (3). We can now examine MacKay's model in reference to my postulate that the system is goal-directed, maximizing the probability that a matching of the received signals and the programed state occurs. MacKay envisages a self-organizing system in which the mismatch signal automatically adjusts a series of control links governing the effectors, so that successful sub-routines of activity become more likely to be tried again while unsuccessful ones become less frequently essayed. Consequently the system evolves modes of activity according to their relative success, and diminishes the occurrence of activities which have not been frequently successful. Thus we get negative feedback control in the system, with the output acting on the field to correct the state of the system in reference to a goal programed in the control element. The feedback operates by means of the mismatch–match signals transmitted through the receptors, and increases

---

[1] Receptor = P; control = C; effector = R; field = E.

Basic Information-flow Design for Self-stabilizing Self-organizing Systems 9

the probability that the match, rather than the mismatch, signal obtains. By extrapolating from MacKay's scheme, we can represent his chart isomorphically with figure (4):

(10)

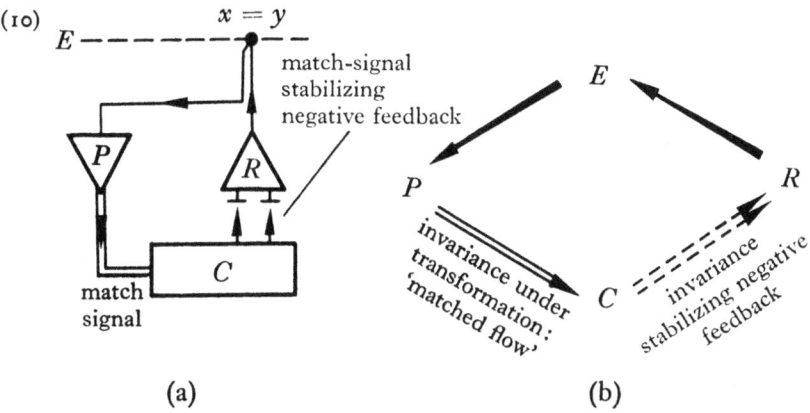

Such feedback-controlled systems order their environment in reference to their incorporated control-codes. (The simplest example of such a system is the room thermostat which manipulates the air temperature of the room in reference to its setting.) We may speak of the system 'projecting' its codes (settings) into the relevant state of the environment. For example, MacKay's system includes a control code programed for the reduction and ultimately the elimination of the differential between points x and y in its field. It can be said to 'project' its code ($x = y$) into its field, since it maximizes the chances that such a state is brought about. (When the state *is* brought about, a match-signal occurs, which is negative feedback-stabilized in subsequent operations.)

To complete the system's description, we must consider its adaptive self-organization, in virtue of which it not only projects its codes into the environment, but maps a changing environment into its codes. Non-adaptive systems may have a running representation of those features of the environment for which they have been programmed and which they have managed to bring about (e.g. the thermostat, which has a 'representation' in its setting of the room temperature which it stabilizes accordingly). However, adaptive systems must also be capable of producing representations of *new* environmental states in their codes. They must be able to 'adapt' to changing surroundings. For such adaptation it is necessary that the system should undertake 'abstract' operations, exploring potential codes for their adequacy to match the new environmental states. Such operations (as we shall soon see in regard to Wiener's 'checker-playing learning machine') are entirely feasible in an artificial system. MacKay assumes that it is possible and normal for some of the internal organizing mechanisms to 'run free' in the absence of excessive stimulation (signal activity). Merely a flexible inhibitory mechanism is necessary to prevent such free-running activity from affecting the effectors. Internal goal-guided activity can then take place which pursues the goal abstractly, that is, purely in terms of the intrinsic capacities (degrees of freedom) of the system. Hypotheses, MacKay points out, are such free-running sub-routines, which refer to features of the environment *if* they are true. Now (to develop these notions further), free-running activities are positive feedback effects, evolving the system from its previous mismatched flow to a potential matched flow. The testing of the new codes for matches with the input involves the active circuit which conduces signals to the receptors. If these match the new codes, the system switches to negative feedback and establishes the codes as an operational program. Thus the system 'confirms' a correlated state of its environment in its control element. The following isomorphism obtains then between the extrapolated state of MacKay's system and figure (5):

(11)

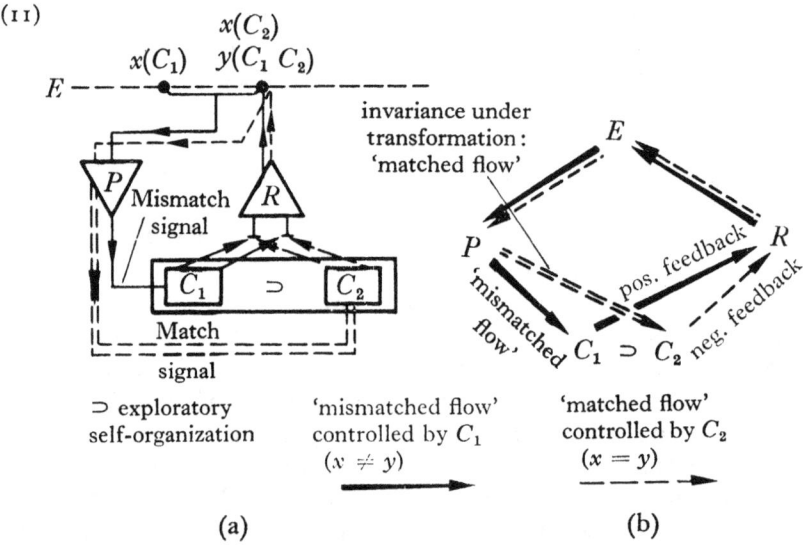

The above chart also gives the basic information-flow of the 'learning machine' described by Wiener in the following example:[1]

[1] Norbert Wiener, 'The Monkey's Paw' in *Management and the Computer of the Future*, ed. Martin Greenberger, MIT Press, 1962.

Basic Information-flow Design for Self-stabilizing Self-organizing Systems 11

'Take the learning machine as it now exists. One form of it is a machine for playing checkers. Now, it is possible to play checkers with machines that are not learning machines. It is possible to write down at any stage of a game all the successive moves that are legally possible for the next stage; to rank them on a scale of values involving loss of pieces, mobility, control, and many other factors . . .; and then give these factors certain weightings, established at the beginning. This procedure leads to a machine that is a checker-playing machine to a limited extent, but not a learning machine. If you were to play against this machine, it would feel like a rigid personality . . . When a rigid personality makes a blunder, it always repeats the same blunder in the same situation. A machine with a less rigid personality can be achieved as follows. The machine plays as before, but now keeps a record of all plays made and all games played. At intervals it is run in a different way. Instead of evaluating moves in terms of a fixed scale of evaluation, it evaluates the scale of evaluation in terms of the games played. It determines which scale of evaluation would have led to wins more assuredly than any other. There are various tricks of accomplishing this which I need not describe here; they are not perfect, but they are valid. The machine, having determined which scale of evaluation would have been most conducive to winning, adopts it for further play. That is learning.'

The 'checker-playing machine' is programed to win the game. It has codes interrelating the signals from its receptors with its responses ('moves') so that the winning situation is progressively realized in its environment (on the 'field' of the checker board). The codes are integrated into a scale of evaluation referring to all possible legal moves, and the response is designed to maximize the chances of selecting the winning move. That is, if the scale of evaluation is correct, the machine wins: the signals conduced by its receptors match its codes. That is the ordinary 'non-learning' machine. In our terms, it is a self-stabilizing but not a self-*organizing* system. It has a 'rigid personality': if the scale of evaluation breaks down, the machine loses the game. Here the scale of evaluation is C, and the successful move (conducing to winning the game) is R, sensed as a match-signal between P and C (the perceived move is a transformation of the code, which represents the winning stratagem). Now, if the system is a '*learning*-machine' it can also be run in a different way. Instead of actually correlating input with output, it can explore an optimum scale of evaluation in free-running activities, limited only by the machine's degrees of freedom. The scale of evaluation which would lead to wins with greater probability than any other is its 'hypothesis': C_2. The machine can be run with the new scale of evaluation and programed so, that if it actually wins games with more regularity with the new than with the old scale, it adopts the new scale for further play. That, as Wiener points out, is learning. It issues in the machine's adaptive organization to conditions in its 'environment' (on the checker-board field, as conditioned by the opponent's moves). Such adaptively self-organizing 'learning machines' can be—and to some extent already have been—produced: the 'tricks' of accomplishing are not perfect, but they are *valid*.[1]

Hence, at least in principle, the here proposed information-flow of adaptive self-organization can be realized in artificial control systems, regardless of whether the systems are programed to win games of checkers or achieve other, perhaps more important tasks.

II

The exploration of the above 'simplest possible scheme for the derivation of invariances from a fluctuating variable world' in terms of MacKay's information-flow design emphasizes that the system makes no reference to entelechies or other principles which could not, *in principle*, be reproduced in artificial regulatory systems. The importance of this claim emerges in view of the next contention: that such systems are *de facto* embodied in biological organisms. Thus, if both claims are justified, the regulatory systems embodied in biological organisms can, in principle, be reproduced in artificial systems—no reference to *sui generis* biological and vitalistic factors or components is required.

The system is, in virtue of its manipulative and adaptive functions, self-stabilizing and self-organizing. It derives 'message' from 'noise' by manipulatively 'projecting' its codes into the environment and adaptively 'mapping' the environment into its codes. Such apparent purposiveness does not presuppose a conscious entertainment of purpose. As Sommerhof has shown, phenomena of adaptive self-regulation can be accounted for in terms of 'directive correlation' which is 'a physical property which can exist in a closed physical system without presupposing the presence within that system of a rational agent and of conscious mental processes.'[2] Biological organisms taken individually are open systems, but the organism/environment field constitutes a system which, for purposes of quasi-purposive adaptation, may be conceived as a directively correlated closed

---

[1] One such machine is Ashby's 'homeostat.' It adapts itself by trial and error to its environment. After a critical value is passed, the machine starts off in a new way of behavior (governed by a new set of differential equations). When it locates a pattern through which it no longer comes into conflict with its environment, it settles into the corresponding state.

[2] G. Sommerhof, *Analytical Biology*, Chapter II. *op. cit.*

system. In that system conscious mental processes functioning as agents pursuing deliberate ends and purposes are not excluded but appear as special—and rather exceptional—cases of directively correlated adaptive processes. The 'focal condition' of a given correlation replaces the teleological notions 'goal,' 'end' or 'aim' in regard to adaptive and purpose-like behavior in biological systems.[1]

The 'goal' of specifically programed feedback stabilization processes, as well as the 'goal' of particular adaptive self-organization functions, can be envisaged as the focal condition of corresponding directive correlations in the biological organism/environment field. Genetically evolving adaptation and individual negative feedback self-stabilization are the basis of all life phenomena. I need not go into much detail on this score, since the evidence is overwhelming and uncontroversial. One can refer to almost any work on the evolution of the species to substantiate the notion that species adapt themselves to their environmental niches by producing mutations the values of which are naturally selected; and one can likewise consult any book on the control processes of individual organisms to appreciate the fact that they depend in their moment-to-moment and day-to-day existence on feedback-stabilized interactions with their environments. As one biologist points out, 'feedback function is not only essential to life as we know it but also . . . this function is the *main* foundation of the life process.'[2] He further shows that feedback stabilization is already exhibited by the virus which is lifelike in its actions only when it is coupling events in the manner that is typical of feedback circuits and that cells, bacteria, and of course all higher forms of organism manifest, and essentially depend on, feedback control.

In applying the principles of our postulated control system to biology, we must identify its functions and components with natural entities and events. Thus the symbol E stands for 'natural environment': the source of all information for the organism. P is the perceptual sensing apparatus of the given organism. It is a filtering mechanism which transmits certain energy radiations ('information') from the environment and excludes others. It ranges from the primitive chemical reactivity of Protozoa, limited to a small range of changes occurring in the immediate proximity of their surface, to the sensitivity of vertebrates and other higher forms of life to a wider range of events occurring at some distance from the organism. C is

---

[1] Sommerhof, *op. cit.*

[2] Robert W. Thornton, 'Integrative Principles in Biology' in *Integrative Principles in Modern Thought*, ed. Margenau (in press). Similar statements are found in Miller ('The Organization of Life'), Cannon (*The Wisdom of the Body*), Wiener (*The Human Use of Human Beings*), et al.

the full organic (where developed: nervous) conducing network as it transmits, and in transmission transforms, signals received from the environment. R signifies the coordinated environment-directed but self-regulative response of the organic system to its sensed information, in virtue of the latter's channelling through C. The system as a whole represents the organism: no sharp dividing line can be drawn for biological self-regulating systems between the organic boundaries and the relevant environment. Functionally, the latter is a component in the former.

When the input matches the codes, biological organisms are in stationary states. Their environmental transactions are negative-feedback stabilized to maintain the match. But when the input passes beyond a critical value, yet remains within the threshold of adaptability of the organisms, the latter switch to positive feedback and evolve new, better adapted states. If they attain such states, the organisms revert to negative feedback to maintain the parameters of the new (quasi-stationary) states. Such feedback-controlled environment-organism transactions become the province of the nervous system in higher forms of life, where precise coordination and control is a precondition of survival. The nervous system of animals tends to be highly developed since animals, unlike plants, cannot make their own food and must actively search for it. Securing the correct match between their organic norms and the signals which inform them of the relevant conditions in the environment involves making frequent and rapid adjustments. Satisfying this requirement presupposes a highly evolved control element in the organism; and this is the nervous system. (The outer box in figure (11), which self-organizingly evolves, if needed, C_1 from C_2.)

The manipulative function of self-stabilizing and self-organizing systems is exhibited by most organisms in conditioning their environment. By building nests, digging burrows, and ultimately working the land and building cities, organisms adapt their environments to themselves. In terms of my scheme, they manipulate E in function of obtaining P's which corresponds to their actual C's. But the environment is never entirely constant and already the manipulative activity of different organisms in one habitat produces changes in it. Hence adaptation is constantly called for. The requirement is satisfied by all adaptable species in seeking out their particular niche and adapting themselves to the conditions there. In addition to such long-term adaptations we can also note empirically 'learned' instances: the ongoing mappings of the relevant environmental events in the nervous system of the more evolved and adaptable organisms. The adaptability of living organisms is vast: most species, other than certain insects (some of which appear to have stabilized their mode of existence for as much as 25 million years) are, in Julian Huxley's terms, 'bundles of adaptation.' Their manipulative capacity is also immense: here the most striking example is provided by our own species. The negative feedback self-stabilizing and positive feedback self-organizing activity pattern of organisms exemplifies the principal features of my basic scheme. By both adaptively and manipulatively matching the signals received from the environment with their codes, living organisms extract the relevant 'message' from the fluctuating 'noise' provided by their environments: they ensure their organic compatibility with their surroundings.

I now turn to my third contention, to wit, that the basic control scheme applies hypothetically to the flow of information in human experience. This book is principally devoted to substantiating this claim. If it succeeds in advancing cogent arguments in favor of the hypothesis, it will have adduced evidence worthy of further study, in the light of which the higher, and hitherto apparently *sui generis*, features of our experience can be assimilated to information-flows in control systems shared, in principle, by artificial systems and *de facto* by living organisms. This type of endeavor is occupying the attention of an increasing number of investigators. General system theorists, systems-analysts, information theorists, cyberneticians and workers in related fields, are becoming more and more aware of the vast philosophical implications offered by the structural-functional, system-analytical approach. The present work wishes to take its place in the growing literature on this field, as a contribution to the elucidation of perceptual, scientific, artistic and religious experience, and of the communication and value of such experience, in terms consistent with control processes both on the biological and on the artificial systems level. The introduction of an isomorphically related hierarchy of circuits will prevent this schematization from falling into the trap of biologistic or physicalist reductionism and at the same time enable it to point out the important connections of so-called mental phenomena with information processing in the worlds of biology and of artificial servomechanisms.

CHAPTER 2

The System-theoretical Analysis of Experience

The ways of interpreting experience are as numerous as the philosophers who have attempted it. Epistemological positions range from solipsistic scepticism to unqualified realism, with side-avenues leading to Platonic rationalism and Bergsonian intuitionism. My particular approach is the system-theoretical one, and the reasons for adopting it need some elucidation. I propose to do this by placing the system-theoretical perspective within the general context of scientific method (of which it is a part) and contrasting it with its most immediately opposing epistemological positions. This exposition is designed merely to show the cogency of undertaking an assessment of human experience in the framework of scientific method, and is not proposed as an outline or description of the latter. The discussion is illustrative rather than demonstrative of the point I wish to make: that human experience can be fruitfully analyzed by recourse to the science-based concepts of system-theory.[1]

I

With the above considerations in mind, let us examine the positions which most directly challenge the empirical and rationalistic system-theoretical one: the position of the radical empiricist and that of the classical rationalist.

The sceptical philosopher, who wishes not to burden his inquiry by presuppositions, will not admit of any notions or ideas as valid unless and until he has found justification for them in his experience. Such a philo-

[1] A further point will emerge in the course of this exposition: that the analysis of experience in reference to the concepts of system-theory coincides with my information-flow design of self-stabilizing self-organizing systems. This point cannot be presupposed, however, but must be permitted to manifest itself in the logical course of the argument.

sopher imposes a two-fold restriction on his inquiry: first, he makes experience into 'my' experience (since everyone else is but an item of 'my' experience and has to be justified by it); and second, he excludes any items of knowledge, such as ideas, thoughts, concepts, or hypotheses, which do not rest on the evidence of his ('my') experience. The sceptical restriction has been introduced into philosophy in systematic form by Berkeley, Hume and Descartes, and finds its most qualified contemporary expression in phenomenology. I shall call this the *empiricist* approach to experience, in the 'radical' sense.

There is also a directly contrary approach to experience. This holds that the laws of thought, the ways in which human beings join together ideas, are the necessary or only guarantee of the truth of our knowledge. The world may be known in just so many ways, and the fact that we know it in these ways systematically and coherently constitutes a system of knowledge, which coincides (in one manner or another) with the system of the world which we know. Whether the ways in which we know the world are determined by our acquaintance with ideal and pure Forms or prototypes of things, or whether they are incorporated in our mind as its *a priori* structure, the laws of thinking and the laws of being coincide. We know things by the power of our reasoning. With diverse ramifications, this approach to problems of human experience was professed by such, otherwise very different, philosophers as Parmenides, Leibnitz, Plato, Hegel and Kant. We may designate the above approach as *rationalist* in character.

Empiricism and rationalism present fundamental points of departure for inquiries into human experience. But they are alternatives only in their pure or extreme form. Empiricism and rationalism may be combined in inquiries which are empiricist in a new, rationalistically modified sense. These inquiries start with the data of 'my' experience, then, instead of restricting themselves only to the idiosyncrasies of my private world, assume that, given sufficient confirmation by others, 'my' experience signifies a generally occurring event which is, or can be, experienced by anyone in my place (assuming that he has sense organs such as I do). With that, radical empiricism has been transcended on one point. It is fully outstripped by the next step, whereby the rationalistic–empirical investigator proceeds to *postulate* interconnections between the various items of (human) experience. The simplest kind of interconnection may be simply a causal relation. The data of experience may be 'stone' and 'window.' Examining each separately, he could not discover that one has a causal relationship to the other. But when he sees the window shattered and the stone rolling away from it he proclaims that the stone broke the window. He places them into causal relation[1]. He also does further things, namely suggests that the stone must have been in motion, must have had a certain mass and velocity, and that these factors, compared to the thickness and resilience of the window pane, were sufficient to cause the latter to shatter. And there is still more to be said of this kind of postulation. The investigator, if he is a physical scientist, will regard the stone as an energy vector disrupting the pattern of potential energy represented by the window pane. He will find a true causal relationship between stone and window in the sense of thermodynamics: energy increases with the shattering of the window and an irreversible process takes place, as described by the Second Law of thermodynamics. (The irreversibility in question is based on probability: the universe is not likely to exist long enough in its present phase to satisfy the time requirement for the probability that the fragments of the window pane reassemble themselves.)

We have gone a long way beyond the datum of immediate experience. Such experience included no more than the window pane and the stone. The laws of thermodynamics, of probability, the time scale, the concepts of entropy, and vector as well as potential energy, are all items of inference. For the radical empiricist such inference is merely based on the belief in past occasions in which the perceived objects behaved in a similar manner. Even a simple causal relation between two billiard balls was said by Hume to be founded merely on our habit of perceiving them in certain ways in relation to one another. Yet the rationalist–empiricist scientist rationalizes beyond the reach of the Humean objection, and continues to draw always more wide ranging inferences. He may assign spatial and temporal coordinates for calculating the motion of the stone, although he by no means 'experienced' the coordinates themselves, nor is he ever likely to do so. Moreover he considers himself at liberty to choose his system of coordinates, selecting either the simple Cartesian coordinates or, if he prefers, the immensely complex generalized coordinates of contemporary mathematical physics. (He is not at *full* liberty to effect such a choice, of course, but the criteria are not furnished by his experiences. Hence, as regards the latter, he *is* at liberty to choose.) The radical empiricist has been left behind, with the immediate experience of the stone and the remains of the window pane, as the investigation proceeds ever further into the domains of reason. But rationalism is not unfettered: it is compelled to check back again and again with immediate experience. If the calculations are made, involving

[1] The rationalistic-empirical investigator places his rationalistically constructed ideas of 'stone' and 'window' in causal relation, rather than his immediate experience of these things. Here his rationalistic bent implicitly protects him from the sceptic's accusation of fallacy, *à la* Hume.

rationalistic entities such as figures for mass, velocity, trajectory, resilience, potential energy, coordinates, and many others, it should be possible to create a situation where all these things apply. In other words, the investigator should be able to take a stone of just such mass, and throw it, as his calculations tell him to, at a window pane of just the indicated size, thickness and resilience. If the window pane shatters and the stone rolls away, precisely as it did in the first instance, his rationalistic excursions are vindicated. He has 'confirmed' their validity in the given situation. Otherwise he shall have to revise his calculations, or perhaps throw them away.

The point is a simple one. The rationalistic–empirical method is that of natural science. It is empirical, because it starts with observations, and returns to observations for confirmation, and it is rationalistic, because it goes considerably beyond experience to logically postulated entities, such as coordinates, correlation coefficients, mass and many more. It brings empiricism into combination with rationalism. This method has proven to be tremendously fruitful. It has produced theories which have revolutionized our life. Its applications surround us on all sides. We are liberated from the bondage of immediate experience, yet are not turned loose in the infinite paths of pure reason.

There is no categorical reason or argument that would guarantee that this method produces results that are more 'true' than the methods of pure empiricism or rationalism. But no such warranties accompany the investigations of the strict empiricist and rationalist either. And if the proof of the pudding is in the eating, we should opt for the rationalist–empiricist method of natural science: it offers better chances of producing workable and confirmable theories explaining the nature of human experience than any other. And since this is my objective, I shall choose the natural scientific method for its higher probability of leading us to the goal.

Using the method of natural science means that we do *not* start with an absolutely clean slate. We do *not* seek to derive all our theories from the analysis of 'my' experience, but acknowledge that we have reliable information as to what kind of things human beings are, and of what kind of things they have experiences. This information is given to us by successful prior applications of this method, i.e. by the validated theories of the natural sciences.

II

Natural science tells us that our species is the product of a long evolutionary process, and that many of the other products of this process furnish us with our vital environment. Man evolved from the proto-organisms, which formed out of such chemical materials as carbon, hydrogen, oxygen and several other species of atom in the shallow primeval seas, some two thousand million years ago. So did all other known species of organisms—and about a million species of plants and a third as many of animals exist today. An analysis of the human body reveals its atomic composition. Yet the human body is not merely a collection of atoms (some five octillion of them), but exhibits sub-totalities of many kinds. These are hierarchically organized, paralleling the paths of evolution. Atoms are bonded into molecules or crystals, these into molecular aggregates, some of which are self-maintaining and replicating. These 'macro-molecules' are components in the intricate system which makes up the cell, and cells form tissues, organs and, through their mediation, the full organic body. The experience had by a human being is, therefore, the experience had by a hierarchically organized complex of atoms, molecules, crystals, macro-molecules, cells, tissues and organs. But what is this experience an experience *of*? The answer to this is surprisingly simple. It is the experience of *other* complexes of these unities, variously organized. In experiencing you, I experience a hierarchy of atoms, etc., organized very similarly to myself. In experiencing your cat, I still experience such a hierarchy, only to a very small extent less complexly organized (since the cat's central nervous system is less developed). If I experience a mouse, a fish, even a tree or seaweed, the answer remains similar: I experience hierarchies of atoms, molecules, crystals, macro-molecules, cells, tissues and organs, in which, as I go down the scale of evolution, the upper elements are increasingly missing. Thus plants do not have organs, and early organisms (such as the Protozoa) need have neither tissues nor cells as components—they may be composed of a single cell themselves. When I experience an object which is 'not living' (according to ordinary linguistic usage) there is a good chance that I refer to one from which the cell and perhaps even the macro-molecular component has been stripped. Such is the case when I experience much of my surroundings, including rock, air, water, and so on. While I cannot directly experience anything smaller than a considerable chunk of molecules or crystals, due to microscopic scale of size, on analyzing these objects I may cogently infer that they consist of smaller unities, such as atoms, and that these in turn may consist of the problematical phenomena which, for lack of a better term, scientists still refer to as 'elementary particles.' Hence the *objects* of my experience are basically the same as the *subject* of my experience, differing merely in their complexity and form of organization.

I have assumed that the subject of human experience is that complex hierarchy of atoms, molecules, etc., which we denote 'man.' But is this a justified assumption? Is the human body the subject of experience *in toto*? Can we not cogently speak of 'experiencing my hands' and even of 'experiencing the lifting of my hands'? The assumption, that human experience is experience had *by* a member of the human species *of* his environment, does not commit me to regard the total human organism as the subject of experience, as long as experience obtains in virtue of it. The human organism may in fact function as the environment (or part of it) *of* which experience is had. But if so, just who (or 'what') does the experiencing? The little homunculus in the brain; the infamous 'ghost in the machine'? To this we may retort: 'no, the subject of experience is the nervous system operating within the organism and also experiencing the rest of the organism.' With this we should have come closer to giving a satisfactory answer but have not quite given it. For then we should have created a subject in the guise of the nervous system and counterposed it, as to its objects, both to the rest of the organism and the external environment. We would still have our homunculus, only now we would call it 'nervous system.' The solution is both more radical and more simple. We must do away with the subject–object distinction in analyzing experience. This does not mean that we reject the concepts of organism and environment, as handed to us by natural science. It only means that we conceive of experience as linking organism and environment in a continuous chain of events, from which we cannot, without arbitrariness, abstract an entity called 'organism' and another called 'environment.' The organism is continuous with its environment, and its experience refers to a series of transactions constituting the organism–environment continuum.

The elimination of a subject–object dichotomy in this view of experience is directly borne out by its analysis, performed by the methods, and in the light of the previous results, of natural science. In such analysis we do not see a categorical 'I' against a categorically distinct 'you' and 'it' but assess our experience as interweaving, in a complex chain of events, the nervous system, the rest of our body, and our external (i.e. extra-dermal) environment. This chain, of which one section is directly available for introspection, constitutes the full extent of human experience. The present view, far from being mystical, 'far-out' or 'abstract,' is in fact of the utmost simplicity and concreteness. Whitehead insisted upon it with good reason when he rejected the traditional doctrine of experience as constituted by a knower and a known. In his view the 'actual occasion' is both subject and object: these become relative terms. 'An occasion of experience is an activity, analysable into modes of functioning which jointly constitute its processes of becoming. Each mode is analysable into the total experience as active subject, and into the thing or object with which the special activity is concerned.'[1] Whitehead's insight, explored within his inclusive metaphysical scheme, is demonstrably true when we approach the interpretation of our ordinary, everyday experience with the empiricist-rationalist method of natural science. Let me illustrate this claim with a simple example.

Consider the following proposition alternately in the empirical–rationalistic light of scientific evidence and in the introspective optic of radical empiricism: 'Light falls on my eyelids and I open my eyes.' The proposition states an experienced chain of events and is capable of being described by radical empiricist introspection as well as explained by empiricist-rationalistic theory formulation and application. The introspective evidence would state 'I perceived the light.' 'I' is the subject of experience; 'light' the object. Introspection would further suggest that having perceived the light, I decided to open my eyes. The light—the object of the experience—did not dictate my opening my eyes, which was an act performed entirely by me—the experience's subject. Thus the two halves of the experience are effectively separated. (To be sure, one learns to think like this—an infant does not do so. Piaget and other investigators concluded that, in his first weeks of existence after birth, man does not distinguish himself from his extra-dermal environment.)

Without contesting the validity of the introspective evidence for everyday purposes, let us consider the above situation in the light of a scheme derived from a considerable body of scientific evidence. 'Light falls on my eyelids and I open my eyes.' Light-sensitive optical sensors react to an increase in the intensity of the light falling on them. The light rays are converted into nerve signals and are conducted to the brain. There complex operations are set in motion whereby the information is funnelled, sharpened and analyzed. Nerve signals are sent along nervous pathways which activate the muscles of the eyelids; the eyes are opened.

Two sets of descriptions apply to our example. The former comes from radical empiricist introspection; the latter from empirical–rational science. The reason for preferring the latter is its potential fruitfulness: it derives from the vast framework of knowledge accumulated by the previous applications of the method it incorporates and permits us to progress beyond the confines of the introspective portion of human experience. The rationalist-empiricist description has the further advantage of eliminating the subject–object dichotomy. It recognizes neither subject as distinct from object, nor object distinct from subject. It deals with a chain of events which may,

---

[1] A. N. Whitehead, *Adventures of Ideas*, New York 1933, p. 178.

only with some arbitrariness, be analyzed to a 'subject-component' and an 'object-component.'

III

The rationalist–empiricist description of the experience given in my example may be restated in system–theoretical terms, consistently with the basic information-flow design developed in chapter 1. We can designate the events occurring in the optical sensors with the sign P: it stands for 'input.' The events in the nervous system and the reticular regions of the brain will then be symbolized by C, denoting the control-codes interconnecting input and output. And the events making up the opening of the eyelids acquire the sign R, as the relevant response (output) to the coded perception (input). We thus get a linear scheme of events:

(12) $$P \longrightarrow C \longrightarrow R$$

(perception) (codes) (response)

'Perception' does not suggest a complete item of sensory cognition; it is restricted to the sensory signals which, in the above example, signify an increase in the light intensity registered by the eye's optical sensors. This signal is meaningless in itself: the 'codes' which incorporate its significance for the system must be had beforehand. If they are present, the signals are de-coded as 'increased light intensity outside the eyes' and the response which leads to the opening of the eyelids is correlated with it.

So far I have omitted two factors in the described situation: the light which fell upon the eyelids, and the light which was perceived when the eyes were opened. The first came prior to the P in the chain; the second followed the R. Let us denote the light by the letter E: it represents the relevant aspect of the environment. We thus get:

(13) $$E_1 \to P \to C \to R \to E_2$$

E appears in two places but is in fact a single event: the light as related to the other events (sensing, coding, responding). But is the scheme transformable to take account of the singularity of E when it appears on two different occasions? To consider this, let me set forth the proposition. ('Light falls on my eyes, I open my eyes and) see a sunlit tree.' Setting forth our scientific description of the proposition, we get 'upon the contraction of the eyelid muscles a great increase in light intensity is registered by the optical sensors; the appropriate messages are channelled to the brain, are decoded and nerve impulses are sent to the eye muscles to adjust the retina to the given light. Thereby messages are sent along the afferent nerves to the cortical center where they are funnelled, sharpened and analysed and result in a coordinated response appropriate to the significance of "sunlit tree" (this may be to get up and walk away, to turn over and fall asleep, not to do anything for the moment, or anything else).' What in fact happened was that the light, which originally resulted in the opening of the eyes, was hereby perceived in greater detail and analyzed into 'sunlit tree.' This in turn resulted in responses which could prolong, modify or remove the light from the chain of events which makes up the experience. Thus the same light is involved in a continuous circuit of events, involving sensory input, neural coding, and behavioral responding. The thus emerging circuit is identical with my basic information-flow design for self-organizing self-stabilizing systems:[1]

(14)

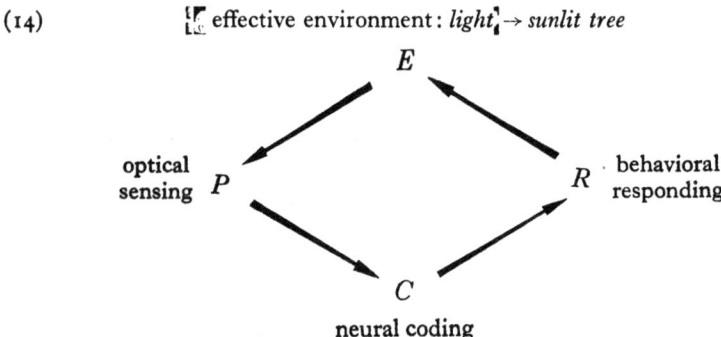

The validity of the scheme is, of course, not confined to the above example. E can stand for any event in the environment which is sensed and the neural signals of which are coded and correlated with behavioral responses. P is not limited to optical sensors in the eye, and not limited even to the five exteroceptive senses. It may refer to organic and kinesthetic sensors as well, conveyors of sensations of muscular tension and relaxation, pains, bodily functions and the general orientation (or 'set') of the organism. If P stands for such proprioceptive sensors, then E represents the 'internal' as opposed to the 'external' environment. (But, as I shall discuss, more than one circuit of information-flow can occur at any given time.) The distinction between subject and object is just as meaningless in regard to organic sensing and internal environment as it is with reference to exteroception and external environment. Reflection will show that it is no more warranted

[1] Cf. figures (1) and (2).

to separate the light falling upon the eyes from the sensing, interpreting and responding in regard to it than it is to separate the sensation of raising my arm from the sensing, interpreting and responding which follows *it*.[1] In each case we get an event affecting sensors, the interpretation of the sensory signals in reference to preestablished codes, and a coordinated response. (A lack of motor activity, if coordinated with sensing and coding, does not mean that there is no response, merely that it is passive in character.)

The continuous chain of events here described obtains in a wide variety of forms and circumstances; the above examples constitute merely a random sampling. The variety is introduced by a chain-reaction when any of the terms (E, P, C, R) is modified. For example, modifying the event denoted E modifies P (the sensing of the event), which in turn is interpreted by a different set of C's and the response, very naturally, will also be different. If, for example, the 'effective environment' is a motorcycle patrolman approaching while I am driving on the turnpike, the P will be my perception of his figure in the rearview mirror. The C's will include a 'code' fixing the speed-limit on the turnpike as I recall it. The R will be my slowing down. By so responding I try to bring myself into a relationship with my effective environment (the patrolman) which corresponds to my recalled C (the speed-limit). I do this because I do not want to be stopped—and perhaps arrested. This means acting in such a manner that my P's should not transform into the figure of the patrolman pulling up alongside and signalling me to stop. A continuous chain of events obtains acting on the environment in accordance with codes and adapting it to my purposes, going through the phases of sensing, interpreting and responding. Essentially the same thing happened in the case of the previous example: by first opening, and then narrowing my eyes to accomodate them to the new level of light intensity in my environment, I have enabled myself to perceive the tree which in turn could lead me to respond in accordance with my wants and motivations. The constant focussing and adjusting of the eyes, in reference to the physiological standards associated with and incorporated in my nervous system, the constant interpretation of the sensory signals which can thus be channelled to my brain for sharpening and analysis, this time in reference to the conscious or semi-conscious criteria of what the tree means to me in the context of my present situation, represents the

[1] I am not reducing introspectively known sensations to objective 'brain events' without qualification, but argue only that rationalist–empiricist natural science can deal with both as correlated elements in a sequence of events involving the organism and its internal and external stimuli. Switching to the 'protocol language' of introspection, the brain-events appear as subjective sensations. Cf. pp. 39–41 below.

way in which I manage to establish, and to maintain, constant and stable relationships with my environment. Extended over a longer period of time, such chains permit me to exist as a purposive human being.

We have now identified, by means of a random sampling of human experience, *the* most basic characteristic of life: *feedback stabilization*. I mentioned the universal applicability of the concept of feedback stabilization in biology in Chapter 1 and shall not belabor the point here. It is important, however, to make sure that we do not reduce the phenomenon of mind to the kind of feedback control system instantiated by biological organisms. In fact, I shall not be guilty of such reductionism. I shall note that the nervous system performs the function of feedback stabilization on more than one level of operation. Natural science investigates primarily the basic, homeostatic level: the empirical disclosure of higher cognitive processes is yet to be effected. And the basic level of homeostatic operation clearly exemplifies the simple feedback scheme I outlined. There we find the *receptors*, conducing afferent stimulation to the system, and the *effectors*, responsible for efference. An incoming energy vector (stimulus, substance, or information carried by these) is picked up by the receptors and results in a stimulation of the effectors. This basic reflex-arc, however, is not sufficient for the self-sustenance of the immensely complex human organism. The proper responses must be coupled to each stimulus and the decision as to the correctness of a response involves a selection between many alternate possibilities. Thus the receptors and effectors are connected through a highly evolved conducing network which sharpens, funnels and analyzes the stimuli and injects autonomous elements into them, ultimately to provide a response which reflects the requirements of the organism even more than the initial properties of the stimulus. The intervening conducing network is the nervous system, including the various regions of the brain. The function of this system is to 'code' the stimuli in reference to the needs and wishes of the organism as a whole. Thus I identify it with the symbol C. Its importance becomes evident when we consider that both the environment, originating the stimuli, and the organism, receiving and transmitting it, are subject to constant (though finite and limited) variation. The stimuli not only change, but also change their significance. The total context changes in which they are received. The proper evaluation of each stimulus is the task of the higher nervous system and the response it produces must be considerably more than a reflex, however conditioned, to the initial stimulation. The essentially linear reflex-arc, even in the case of conditioned reflexes, is inadequate for the purposes of the organism of man, whose complexity involves planning ahead and not only anticipating, but also controlling, the future course of events. Thus the receptors must be supplied with the efferent energies which not only produce the properly coordinated response to a given afferent stimulus, but which also produce further, controlled changes in afferent stimuli. In other words efference must control re-afference: the response to an experience must anticipate and control the course of future experiences. The nervous system does not directly connect efference to re-afference but must pass through an external link which is the *source* of the re-afferent stimulus. This link—which may be the internal (organic) as well as the external (extra-dermal) *environment*, thus becomes a 'built-in' component of the operations. I denote it 'effective environment' (E).

Hence the nervous system controls the behavior of the organism by feedback-stabilizing the organism with its effective environment through the coded correlation of stimulus and response. Thereby the response becomes more than the response *to* the stimulus: it functions as the response of the organism to its specific situation in its environment. This situation has a temporal extension due to the temporally effective feedback control (cf. figure 2). Now, neurophysiology operates with constructs that refer to the physical survival of the organism and finds that feedback stabilization is one of its key constructs. But the fact that the empirical methods of neurophysiology cannot, for the present, penetrate to the more complex mental operations, e.g. those involved in scientific or artistic activity, does not imply that such activities rest on a fundamentally different principle. It only suggests that, in hypothetically extending empirical findings, we must be careful to introduce a distinction between levels. Because, if we fail to do so, biological reductionism results. Such position is implicit in the work of a number of biologists, who view homeostatic self-regulation and purposive mental behavior as identical, or at least as equivalent. For example, Sinnott states that 'the insistent tendency among living things for bodily development to reach and maintain, as a norm or goal, an organized living system of a definite kind, and the equally persistent directiveness or goal-seeking that is the essential feature of behavior, are *fundamentally the same thing*, merely two aspects of the basic regulatory character all living stuff displays.'[1] He quotes Lillie approvingly, who concludes that 'in living organisms physical integration and psychical integration represent two aspects, corresponding to two mutually complementary sets of factors, of one and the same biological process.'[2] This line of thought is eventually led to regard all of psychology as the study of those homeostatic processes which involve the whole organism (Stagner and Karwoski).

[1] E. Sinnott, *The Biology of the Spirit*, New York, 1955, p. 52.
[2] *Ibid*, p. 55.

The danger of failing to differentiate between multiple levels of regulatory activity is clearly exemplified in the conclusion Sinnott is forced to reach concerning the biological basis of conscious behavior. 'Just as the form and character of this mature individual are thus immanent, though yet unrealized, in the egg from which it grows, so, I suggest, a purpose yet to be realized may be immanent in the cells of the brain. Conformity to such a purpose, an act of biological regulation, is the basis of behavior. A *conscicus* purpose is the inner experience of this protoplasmic goal-seeking.'[1] To regard higher mental—including cognitive and aesthetic—purposes as the inner experience of protoplasmic goal-seeking is, as stated, an instance of rampant biological reductionism. To avoid it, without breaking the continuum of the biological and the psychological, one must be careful to point out, and demonstrate, that the basic feedback cycle manifested by viruses, bacteria, cells and other biochemical agents, is the manifestation of but one level of feedback that operates in regard to living things. It is an important one, because on it depend such basic life processes as homeostasis and reproduction. (These are but special cases of the feedback circuitry; ones which are specifically directed toward the attainment of particular ends.) However, such feedback is by no means the very same that operates when I slow down to avoid getting a speeding ticket and is only partially the same as the one which is effective when I open my eyes when light falls on my eyelids and see a tree. The terms E, P, C, R, are variable; it is only their relationship which is constant. It is feedback which operates, I shall argue, as I write these lines and think these thoughts, but the E's, P's, C's, and R's are not merely those found in physiological feedback: they are *those as well as others*.[2]

A systems–analytical theory of mind that recognizes but a single level of feedback is crassly mechanistic and naïvely reductionist. But one which recognizes multiple feedback circuits, hierarchically organized and isomorphically related may well succeed in giving an adequate non-reductionist explanation of typically mental phenomena in direct reference to the biological foundations of life. The task is to outline the *structure* of human experience; a structure which holds true on all its levels in virtue of the isomorphic relation of its components. It is this structuralist and system–analytic—but also Whiteheadian—goal which I pursue in the next chapter.

---

[1] *Ibid*, p. 56.

[2] I am not suggesting that the cognitive levels are not functions of neurophysiological brain-processes (cf. the Appendix), only that these processes are different from, and irreducible to, physiological homeostasis.

CHAPTER 3

Levels of Controlled Information-flow in Experience

We considered various modes of approaching the interpretation of human experience; have opted for the method of natural science; and on sampling experience within the framework afforded by past applications of this method found that the basic information-flow design developed in Chapter 1 is applicable to it.

We thus uncovered the conceptual link of human experience and biological as well as artificial feedback systems. Our task can be envisaged therefore as the exploration of the multiple levels of human experience within this integrative conceptual framework.

I shall now carry out this program by proposing models for the different levels of human experience. Each model, presented as an information-flow chart, conserves the basic relationships outlined in figures (1) through (7). Differences among them, amounting to differentiations of levels, will be introduced by the specific values assumed by the invariantly related terms. Thus each level will represent a particular transformation of the invariance embedded in their common structure. This invariance furnishes us with the unifying nexus of human experience and other, biological and physical phenomena. The levels I shall discuss are the following: L_0 *Homeostatic Feedback*; L_1 *Sensory Feedback*; L_2 *Meta-Sensory Feedback*. Within the latter I shall distinguish: L_{21} (*science*); L_{211} (*art*); and L_{2111} (*religion*).

I Homeostatic Feedback: L_0 (Physiological Activity)

Under 'homeostatic feedback' I shall understand the self-stabilizing and self-organizing processes of the human (as well as animal) body. I take the body as providing the 'effective environment' in the context of which specific regulatory functions take place. This requires a conceptual abstraction from the relations of the body to its extra-dermal environment, i.e.

from the organism/environment field. But this abstraction will be made good in the subsequent analyses, where the relations of the body to its outside environment will be specifically considered.[1] The levels of operation of the human organism are multiple, and their analysis involves performing such 'idealizations' as the present. In virtue of it, the fundamental control scheme, represented in the basic information-flow charts proposed in Chapter 1, can be discovered on various levels, and the levels can be interrelated through their structural isomorphisms.

The most basic of the levels of controlled information-flow in the human organism is the one which regulates and maintains its internal states in reference to its incorporated norms. I shall designate this level the homeostatic one, constituting the organism's physiological pattern of activity.

Bertalanffy, who presents the 'simplest feedback scheme' as follows,[2]

(15)

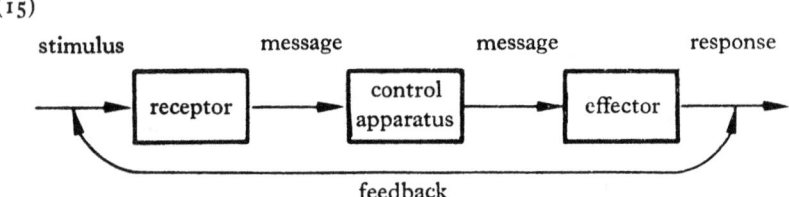

points out that in application to the living organism, the scheme represents the concept of *homeostasis*. Homeostasis is the ensemble of organic regulatory functions which maintain the stationary states of the organism around its intrinsic norms. I shall show that homeostasis in this sense exemplifies the basic information-flow design given in figures (1) through (4).

If we take Bertalanffy's simple feedback model and apply it to the homeostasis of the body, we must add what Claude Bernard called the *'milieu intérieur'* to the scheme. The 'internal environment' is the source of the stimulus reaching the organic receptors as well as the object of the response by the regulative effectors. It thus figures in two places in the scheme: prior to *stimulus*, and following *response*. By noting the internal environment with the letter E, we get the basic information-flow design (fig. 16). Here E functions as the link completing the feedback loop. This link is the complete human (animal) organism as it originates stimuli signalling its states, and receives regulative directives bringing about the conform-

[1] Pp. 36 ff.
[2] L. v. Bertalanffy, 'General System Theory—A Critical Review,' *General Systems*, VII (1962).

ity of its states with the norms incorporated in the 'control apparatus' (nervous system).

(16)

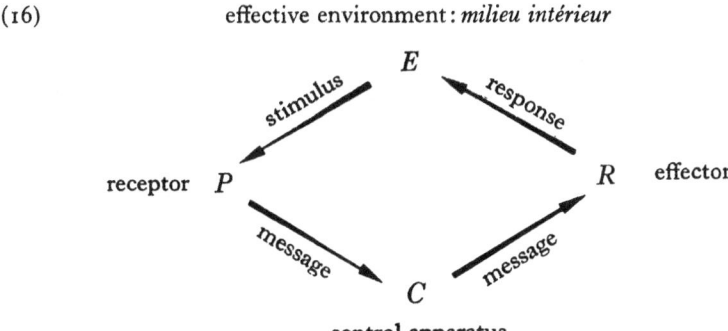

The information-flow of homeostasis may be described in the following terms. A given event in the organism (this can be anything from indigestion to sexual excitation) is proprioceptively sensed ($E \to P$). The signal itself is merely an electro-chemical discharge, meaningless in the absence of an incorporated code which couples it to the proper response. The coupling is accomplished by means of the nervous system, whereby the signal is integrated with other signals in the reticular formations of the brain and the summated impulses are either conduced to the cortical regions where they are sharpened and analyzed, or give rise to organic responses directly. In either case, the proprioceptive stimulus constitutes a 'message' sent to the control center, where it is coupled, in reference to the codes of the center, with specific regulatory responses ($P \to C$). The 'message' interconnecting the control center and the effector mechanism gives the

(17)

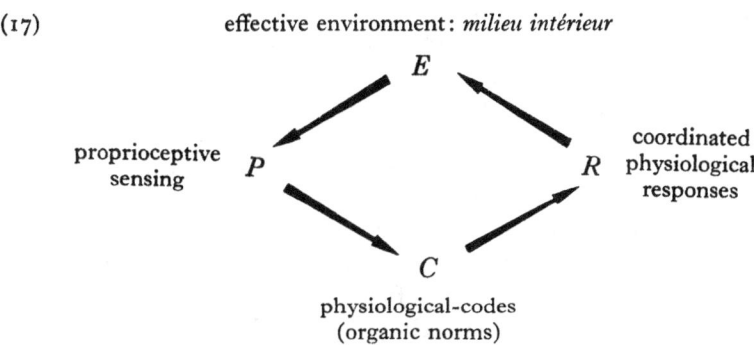

L_0, *general information-flow*

passage ($C \to R$). The effectors fulfill the regulatory functions which maintain the internal environment around the organic norms of the system ($R \to E$). The thus regulated bodily environment is the source of further stimuli ($E \to P$). Thus the circuit is set forth in a continuous cycle.

Figure (17) restates figure (16) in terms of this interpretation of homeostasis. The 'physiological-codes' (or 'organic norms') function as the criteria defining the *goals* of given homeostatic processes. These goals do not imply the conscious entertainment of purpose and do not represent the final causes of the processes directed toward attaining them. They are more cogently considered to be the focal conditions of directive correlations in the organic system.[1] The focal conditions are particular stationary states of the internal environment; those which correspond to the norms incorporated in the nervous system. The particular homeostatic process operates so as to attain the programed goals: that is, P and R are so coupled by C that R leads to the desired state of E. Constant reference to P 'checks up' on the progress and corrects the cycle for errors. This is the task of proper and flexible coding. A successful cycle attains its goal, e.g. maintains the constancy of the internal environment, heals wounds, and generally maintains the organism in its appropriate stationary state.

The examples of homeostasis are legion. If the oxygen content of the air in the lungs decreases, the supply of red corpuscles in the blood increases through the hypertrophy of the erythron. If the oxygen content of the air increases, the erythrocites decrease. When the organism's water input is reduced, pituitrin is secreted which has an anti-diuretic effect and checks the output of water through the kidneys. When the water supply is replenished, pituitrin secretion is inhibited and output through the kidneys becomes accelerated. If any of several substances (such as protein, fat, calcium, etc.) are not supplied through the usual channels, stores of these substances are released. If skin-temperature drops, body-heat is generated by a higher rate of heart beat through increased blood sugar and sympathetico-adrenal action; the same effect is also produced by automatic muscular action such as shivering. If skin-temperatures increase, sweat is produced, the evaporation of which reduces body-temperature. By means of such physiologically coded proprioception-response patterns essential constancies are maintained in the human organism's *milieu intérieur*. These include blood pressure, the oxygen content of blood (Cannon enumerates no less than fourteen homeostatic processes directed toward this goal alone), water content (which is independent of actual water intake and output up to three days), the supply of sugar, salt, protein, and fat, and so on.

[1] Cf. Ch. 1.

The goal (focal condition) of physiological feedback circuits may also be the reestablishment of a state of E which has been damaged by external agency. I am referring to the processes of healing and regeneration. The introduction of a sharp blade or of excessive heat to a part of the body results in a wound, signalled by the proprioceptive sensors as pain. Complex responses are coupled to these signals, including the instantaneous withdrawal of the exposed part from the wounding agent (e.g. the reflexive snatching of one's hand from a hot surface). Further signals activate cells in the area bordering the wound. Through division, a sufficient number of cells is produced, and by means of still imperfectly understood processes channelled along to the wounded area, to provide a covering of sufficient density. Epidermal cells form a covering layer which is thicker than will be eventually needed, and when the cuticle has formed this layer thins out by cell degeneration to the correct density. The healing cycle is completed when a normal layer of skin has formed. The end of such feedback-cycles (which are by no means limited to the healing of surface wounds) is the reestablishment of the pre-damaged stationary state of the *milieu intérieur*.

Homeostasis, healing, as well as the 'general adaptation syndrome' (G.A.S.) represent feedback circuits programed to maintain and reestablish the stationary state of E. The coupling of sensing and response patterns defines this state as the goal toward which the organism tends, within certain limiting conditions (beyond which sickness or death results). Now, the G.A.S. operates, unlike healing, by involving the entire organism in the self-maintenance directed feedback cycle. Selye defines stress as 'the state manifested by a specific syndrome which consists of all the nonspecifically induced changes within a biologic system.'[1] Stress is used as the common denominator of all adaptive reactions in the organism. Selye distinguishes two types of change in the stress reaction: the primary change, nonspecific both in form and in causation, and a secondary change, which manifests the specific pattern of the general adaptation syndrome. The first type of change triggers the second. The latter consists in three stages: the 'alarm reaction,' the 'stage of resistance,' and the 'stage of exhaustion.' Virtually every organ and chemical constituent of the organism participates in this tri-phasic stress reaction. The process occurs in the presence of a 'stressor,' which functions as a state of E; the reaction is a tri-phasic feedback process adapting the organism, through sensing, interpreting and responding, to the stressor. For example, if the body is exposed to cold (a stressor), the adrenal cortex first discharges the available fat-granules which contain the cortical hormones (alarm reaction); then it

---

[1] Hans Selye, *The Stress of Life*, Toronto, 1956, p. 54.

becomes laden with an unusually large number of fat-droplets (stage of resistance), and, if exposure continues, the fat-droplets are lost (stage of exhaustion). The stress-syndrome thus represents the general adaptation of the entire organism to critical conditions. In virtue of the feedback cycle controlled by the general nervous system, the stressor is adequately responded to through a series of new quasi-stationary states until such time as the adaptive potentials of the organism are exhausted (Selye speaks of the exhaustion of 'adaptation energy'). At each stage the stressor is proprioceptively sensed, and the adaptive responses are coordinated through the intrinsic physiological reaction patterns developed in the nervous system.

The specific goals—or focal conditions—of homeostasis may vary. The general character of such goals remains the same, however: it is the realization, in the internal environment, of steady-states the norms of which are encoded in the nervous system. To use the language of our self-stabilizing system, we can say that, in its codes or norms, the nervous system maintains a running representation of the body's states, and coordinates input and output in function of projecting its representations into the internal environment. Under the general notion of physiological-code we may include the various normative processes of a living human organism including not only moment-to-moment self-regulation, but also growth, development and reproduction. This assessment agrees with Sinnott's view, that all basic biological processes represent forms of homeostasis.[1]

Homeostatic processes stabilize the internal environment around the intrinsic codes (norms) of the organism. Such processes may be represented by the following diagram:

(18)

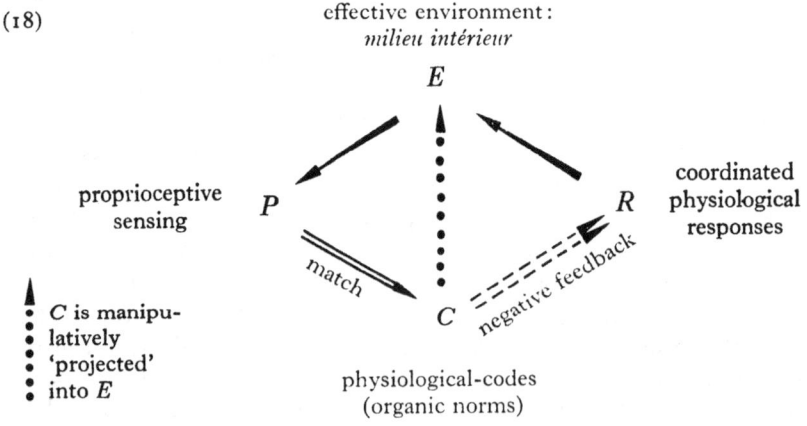

L_0 *manipulative self-stabilization*

[1] Sinnott, *op. cit.*

A sensory signal conducing information relevant to the internal environment represents a transformation of the invariant code when the internal environment maintains normal conditions. The coupling of these signals with the response patterns is thus correlated that the probability of achieving a 'match' is optimized. As a result, when successful, the homeostatic control circuit negative feedback stabilizes the internal environment around the intrinsic organic norms (projects C into E). This is what we mean by 'bodily health' and 'normalcy.' That state is a normative steady-state in the organism.

But the human body not only stabilizes itself around its intrinsic norms but (within limits) also evolves such norms which best fit changing conditions in E. The adaptive self-organization of the organism is illustrated in the next diagram:

(19)

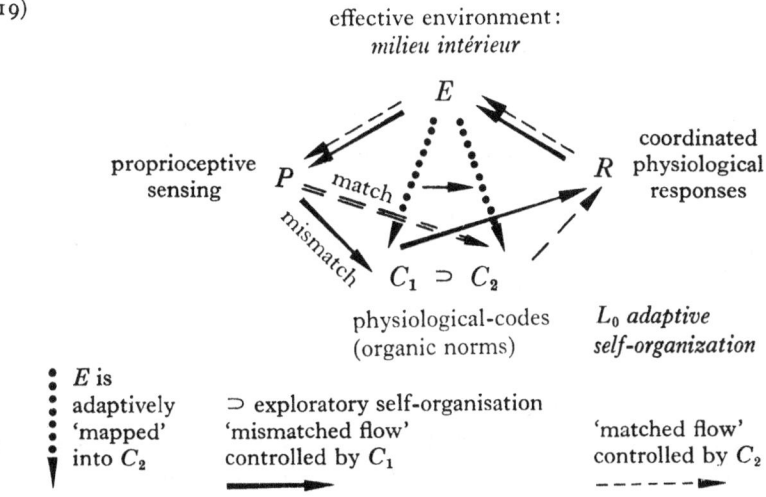

Here we must keep in mind that, on the level of homeostasis, the adaptive self-organization of the organism (the mapping of a changed E into C_2) is mostly a genetic process, due to imperfectly self-replication and thus mutating genes. The exploratory activity of the organism (its free-running functioning) is dictated by the degrees of freedom incorporated in its genetic information pool. The mutations, when produced, are tested by natural selection, i.e. by the functional potentials of the new mutant code to optimize the occurrence of organic signals which match it (i.e. fall within its range of invariance). Hence new and better adapted species can evolve, correlating input and output by codes which function as increasingly successful organic norms. For a given individual physiological adaptation is limited: C_2 could only define a new quasi-stationary state, compatible with those typical of the species, but better adapted to actual conditions (e.g. the stages of alarm and resistance of the stress-syndrome).

Homeostatic feedback is not infused with self-awareness except in some of its phases (pains, excitations, and so on). It nevertheless forms the foundation of human experience in that it constitutes what scientists and philosophers call the 'body scheme' or the organic 'set': the ground upon which rest, in higher level reflective and cognitive processes, the feelings of the *self*.

II Sensory Feedback: L_1 (Perceptual-Cognitive Activity)

The self-stabilizing feedback of an organism deals with the region of the body as with a closed system, undergoing changes. The changes are externally induced, however, and if precise control over the internal environment is to be maintained, the external agencies will have to be taken into account. Thus the organism must constitute its regulative processes in view of the fact that it is an environmentally interacting *open* system.

The cognizance of an external agency as productive of changes in the internal environment ranges from the limited sensory capacities of Protozoa to the highly accurate exteroceptive organs of higher forms of life. The latter are evolved when some cognizance of external agency, causing organic changes of state, becomes a precondition of survival. For example, molluscs, marine plants and other primitive forms of life get along with a largely intra-organic regulatory mechanism: food is wafted to them by the surrounding medium and their waste products are disposed of in a similarly convenient fashion. Consequently it is sufficient for their purposes that they sense their own states and operate the regulative responses coupled to these stimuli through their organic codes. They need not acquire an 'insight' (as Thorpe defines the term) into relationships in their extra-dermal environment: that environment functions merely as the release stimulus of defensive and regulative reactions, being the 'noumenal' realm beyond the organic states which are directly sensed. However, the limitations of a purely homeostatic feedback-stabilization, for the purposes of such complex organisms as the human, soon become apparent. Homeostatic mechanisms are not surrendered, but become components in exteroceptive, extra-dermal environment encompassing regulative circuits, making the human being a *multilevel* feedback controlled system.

Consider that in the embryonic stage the mother's womb provides the developing human organism with all its requirements, much as the sea provides for the needs of primitive marine life. The embryo has no need to perceive, or otherwise to take cognizance of relationships in its extra-dermal environment, since it need not produce coordinated responses in regard to it. But this convenient situation changes soon after birth. The extra-dermal environment becomes much less cooperative, and behavioral responses are gradually but increasingly called for. A perceptual cognition of the extra-dermal realm becomes a precondition of survival. For example, the proprioceptive sensation of hunger proves to be incapable of satisfaction by the sucking and ingestion responses of the infant. Between efference and re-afference there is a missing link, located in the external environment (the mother's breast or the bottle). Thus self-regulation is beyond the control of the purely homeostatic circuit: it demands a *perceptual–cognitive* circuit. A process of learning is called for, a knowledge of the environment beyond the organic boundaries. As Piaget maintains, this empirical knowledge depends upon the awareness of the implicative relations of the elements of the system which demands completion.[1] In the above example, the circuit can be completed by learning to discern the mother's breast and coupling to it the response (the activation of the sucking and ingestion mechanism).

This is the basic step in the development of suprahomeostatic, i.e. perceptual–*cognitive* activity. Upon it follow a continuous series of adaptations and manipulations in regard to the extra-dermal environment, whereby intelligence crystallizes. Piaget emphasizes that an exact definition of intelligence is problematic because it is essentially continuous with sensori-motor and biological adaptive functions, out of which it develops. Problem, hypothesis and control, he goes on to say, whose combination is the mark of intelligence, already exist in embryo in the needs, the errors, the empirical test characteristics of the least developed sensori-motor adaptations. Intelligence crystallizes as the child learns to coordinate perception with externally directed behavior, and repeats bodily movements in anticipation of a desired result. Stages of the development include accommodation of the perceptive organs to follow objects and learning to distinguish the latter despite motion and foreground and background patterns. Awareness of shape and size evolves by means of the development of perceptual constancies incorporating what Piaget calls 'secondary schemata' into the basic scheme. As further schemata are incorporated, the environmental world of spatial and temporal objects is gradually constituted, with the organism detached from it as the 'self.'

[1] Cf. Jean Piaget, *The Psychology of Intelligence* (1966), and other writings.

I shall restate the argument now in terms of information-flow circuits. In doing so I adopt the standpoint of the external analyst, rather than of the experiencing subject. Thus I can talk about circuits and their closure by means of further circuits: the experiencing subject knows only perceptions and responses. I suggest, then, that the basic homeostatic circuit becomes partially inoperative when responses directed toward the internal environment fail to connect with (i.e. feed back to) proprioceptive sensations. (In our example, the infant's sucking and ingestion response fails to issue in the sensation of satisfaction, leaving that of hunger unaffected.) The 'missing link' (the mother's breast, or its substitute, the bottle) lies beyond the internal environment and presupposes the functioning of exteroceptive sensors to locate and incorporate. The use of these sensors calls into play a new circuit which is no longer purely homeostatic in nature, but becomes perceptually *cognitive*. It is through a cognition of the extra-dermal realm that the missing links in homeostatic circuits can be located and the circuits completed. Such cognition becomes the precondition of the completion of the homeostatic circuit, and it is afforded by sensory perceptions of the external (extra-dermal) environment. Of course, from the immanent viewpoint of the experiencing subject, such cognition is an inference from perceptions: what he knows is not the E, but the P's as 'being had of' the E. In cybernetical terms, in the circuit C elicits R when P, regardless of E, which functions merely as the precondition of P. Thus, while the subject implicitly strives to match his codes to his environment, he is only aware of trying to correlate his perceptions and his responses. But the external analyst concludes that when the correlation involves an inferred insight into relations in E, a new level of feedback is operative. This level is perceptually *cognitive*, and is based on operations deserving the name 'intelligence.'

Intelligence is the function of recognizing the data of exteroceptive senses as relationships among environmental entities in definite connection with the self. It presupposes that the exteroceptive data are intelligibly interpreted, i.e. that codes exist whereby given patterns of stimulation 'mean' certain environmental events and that the responses adequate to deal with these events are correlated with them. When P stands for exteroceptive stimuli, E for the external environment (which is presumed to give rise to such stimuli), and R signals the coordinated behavioral responses of the organism to its external environment (on the basis of information in P), the control-element (C) becomes infused with cognitive significance. Such intelligible extra-dermal environment representations I shall call 'sense-codes' or *Gestalten*. They constitute the norms of perceptual intelligibility (fig. 20).

(20)

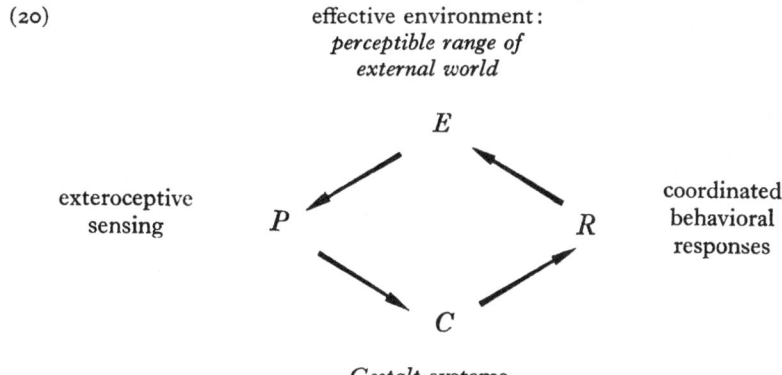

L_1, *general information-flow*

Having reached the level of a cognitive awareness of events, an epistemological problem obtrudes itself, due to the fact that we are, each of us, 'inside' such a cognitive control system as well as, in the present case, adopt the stance of its external analyst. Thus the problem arises that, whereas for the external analyst P is an exteroceptive stimulus, for the introspective subject it is a 'felt' sensation. The traditional problems of 'secondary qualities' such as colors, sounds, smells, tastes and textures, and of 'primary qualities' such as forms of motion, energy states, figure and extension, enter on the scene and require explanation. As long as the datum is not cognized, as it presumably is not in the case of organisms operating purely on the homeostatic level, and as it evidently is not also in our own cases of homeostatic self-regulation, we are not called upon to account for the relationship of a felt sense datum and a conceptualized and constructed event. But in the context of perceptual cognition, we have both a displayed sensory-field and an event 'out there' in the environment (the environment in question may be both extra and intradermal). For example, there is the perceived and introspectively reported 'red patch' and there is the environmental event described by physics as a light source originating radiating energy of a specific wavelength and velocity of translatory motion. Thus redness is a sensation in the mind and it is also an objective event in the environment. To reduce the former to the latter does not make sense, for the sensation 'red patch' has nothing in common with the theoretical constructs of physics. Likewise, the sensation 'indigestion' is not reducible to the malfunctioning of the digestive tract as described in internal medicine[1]. Consequently, rather than *identifying* the perceived and perceptually cognized sensations with objective environmental states, we must content ourselves with postulating their *correlation*. More precisely one may define sensory perception as involving the correlation of felt sensations with transactional states of the organism–environmental continuum. Certain levels and patterns of neural stimulation represent transformations of invariant transactional norms in the organism–environment field, and tactile, kinesthetic, visual, acoustic and other sensations constitute the 'epistemic correlates' of these transformations. To perceive, for example, redness 'out there' (analogously to a stomach pain 'in here') is to obtain a specific relationship between one's nervous system and an energy vector acting on, or in, the organism.

This view accords with Pepper's suggestion that we allow for two perceptual objects: an immediate sensory object which appears in the perceptual field in the shape of sensations, and an ultimate object, which is part of the organism's interactive adjustment to its environment. The immediate qualitative sensory object is tested in reference to the anticipated ultimate object of environmental adaptation. Thus perceptions can be viewed, in Pepper's words, as 'integral segments of our dynamic purposive commerce with our environment.'[2]

The duality of perceptual objects and their importance in confirming the veracity of experience is also brought out by Whitehead, in his notions of perception in the two modes of 'presentational immediacy' and 'causal efficacy.' Presentational immediacy is, for Whitehead, an immediate perception of the contemporary external world, appearing as an element in our experience. The appearance is mediated by qualities, such as colors, sounds, tastes, etc., which can be described with equal truth as our own sensations and as the qualities of the perceived things. In contrast, causal efficacy is a primitive mode of perception, it is the experience of organisms which have 'a sense of the fate from which they emerged and toward which they go'—which 'advance and retreat but hardly differentiate any experience into a presented display.' Causal efficacy is the conformation of the organism to its own past and its own future—that is, to its causally efficacious environment. By a 'symbolic reference' between the two modes— or Pepper's two objects of perception—the various actualities they disclose

---

[1] A case of indigestion may be infused with consciousness, but the homeostatic regulatory processes bearing upon it are not dependent on such awareness. Thus an *awareness* of e.g. indigestion, is an instance of perceptual cognition (cognition of states of the body) rather than a component in the homeostatic circuit.

[2] Stephen C. Pepper, 'A Dynamic View of Perception,' paper delivered at the APA Pacific Division Meeting in 1967. Also see his *Concept and Quality*, La Salle, 1967.

are correlated as elements in our environment. 'Thus the result of symbolic reference is what the actual world is for us, as that datum in our experience productive of feelings, emotions, satisfactions, actions, and finally as the topic for conscious recognition when our mentality intervenes with its conceptual analysis.'[1]

The epistemic correlates of physical energy transfers and information-flows between organism and environment provide the high-grade organism with the means of verifying its experience and correcting its course of action. The two objects of perception (or the two modes of perception) overcome Hume's problem of direct, as opposed to representative perception. The position is based on the hypothesis that when an energy source, within or external to the organism, interacts with its normal processes, the organic or exteroceptive receptors are correspondingly stimulated. The thus produced impulses are integrated with other stimuli transmitted from the remaining receptors, and the summated impulse is conduced to the cortex for analysis. At that moment the sensations constituting the 'proximal object,' or the 'object of presentational immediacy,' appear in the introspectively known field 'consciousness.' In view of the fact that neither can consciousness, and all its component sensations, become an operational construct in the public organism–environment transaction theory, nor can the constructs of that theory be located in our private consciousness, we cannot simply collapse the two kinds of objects or modes of perception into one, but must maintain that a *correlation* exists between them.[2] The introspective 'felt' sensations are the epistemic correlates of energy and information transfers from the viewpoint of the reflective analysis of conscious experience. Whether we speak of sensations or of information-flows depends on the standpoint we adopt. As long as we affirm that both are meaningful but not interreducible concepts, and uphold a correlation and not an identity between them, we are at liberty to pursue our information-flow system-analysis, based on our stated preference for the empirical–rationalistic method of the natural sciences. (cf. Chapter 2.)

The present system–analytical empirical–rational view of perception deals with an information-flow interrelating mind, as the sum of the representations of reality, with the environment, the assumed locus of the external objects. This transactionalist view of mind takes the process of exteroceptive perception and the resulting cognition of the environment as the

---

[1] A. N. Whitehead, *Symbolism, Its Meaning and Effect,* New York: Macmillan Co. 1927, pp. 18–19.
[2] Cf. the writer's *Beyond Scepticism and Realism: A Constructive Exploration of Husserlian and Whiteheadian Methods of Inquiry,* The Hague: Martinus Nijhoff, 1963.

extension of a controlled information-flow circuit to a wider realm of events, whereby that realm is cognized according to the codes of the system, which prescribe its criteria of intelligibility. We perceive the world in terms of its relevance to our codes, and our organization of our sensory data reflects our transactional requirements with the environment. Thus 'the world we experience is the product of perception, not the cause of it' (Cantril), and 'the perceived world pattern mirrors the organized need pattern within' (Murphy). The 'need pattern' is defined by the information-flow design as the mutual adaptation of the environment and the *Gestalt*-systems, so that our perceptions become increasingly intelligible.

An instance of intelligible sensory perception presents us with a configurational form to which purposive response patterns are available. Such forms are invariant when developed, and the data of perception, which fill them with content, function as their particular transformations. I designate these invariant intelligible configurations with the term *Gestalt*. The main body of Gestalt Psychology supports the principle that our organization of the sensory field corresponds to the requirements of intelligibility inherent in relevant *Gestalten* (cf. the 'law of *Prägnanz*'). Perception as well as recall conspire to shape and structure our perceptions in conformance with the 'good' forms of organizations which constitute an intelligible *Gestalt*.[1]

An unqualified assertion, that the content of our sensory cognition is determined by our needs rather than by the environment, may be overstating the case. What we do perceive is, after all, considerably influenced by what is 'out there.' In response to this objection, the 'transactionalist' and 'functionalist' theories of perception, developed by Brunswik, Ittelson, Kilpatrick, Ames, Gibson and others, become relevant. Perception, they tell us, is part of the process of adjustment of organism and environment by means of a continuous series of transactions. The incorporation of 'cues' and 'clues' into the sensory stimulus pattern, by means of past experiences based on need and relevant behavior, enables us to derive a stable world-pattern from the continually shifting kaleidoscopic stimulus pattern delivered by our senses. These theories acknowledge that we do not perceive objects as they are 'out there' (or at least that we cannot know whether we do), but admit that we perceive them in function of their objective relevance to our present needs, past behavior and projects for the future.

Contemporary experimental psychology and empirical neurophysiology make quite clear that our perception of objects is not a mere 'photographing' or 'reflecting' of 'reality' (as Lenin affirmed in the naïve realistic

[1] Cf. K. Koffka, *Principles of Gestalt Psychology*, New York, 1935.

vein). Cognition presupposes recognition: to know something is to refer it to, and identify it by, something known from before. Absence of such reference presents us with an enigma; complete novelty excludes understanding. Our sensory signals are unique and perishing, they fluctuate and never recur in exactly identical forms. To know our P's is to know images in a rotating kaleidoscope. It strains our meaningful use of 'know.' 'Knowledge' implies and presupposes familiarity. And familiarity is impossible in the case of our immediate stream of sensory input, for it exemplifies the Heraclitean river into which one cannot step twice.

This is not to contest that we experience P's and that the P's are had *of* our E ('reality')—it is merely to contest that they constitute the items we *know* in perception. We know not the unique and perishing signals flashing to our mind and changing from moment to moment, but recognizable enduring objects.[1] In recognition of the difficulty, how the flux-world of sense perception can give us such objects, Plato posited his intellectually known domain of universal Forms, and Aristotle underpinned the perceived qualities with an enduring substance. Hume, in objecting to the latter, found himself with an atomic series of sense impressions which pass in review without disclosing whence they came from and what they are. Yet the Platonic alternative overshoots the mark. The Forms constituting our knowledge may be intellectually known, in the sense that they are contributions of our inherently rational physio-perceptual capacities, but they do not, for that reason, need to exist apart. Our sense-objects may be 'localizations of universals,' but they exist in their exemplifications, and apart from them only in our heads, as our familiar *Gestalten*. The latter are combinations of characteristics abstracted, as Aristotle affirms, from previous experiences by means of, as our contemporaries McCulloch and Pitts suggest, processes of 'averaging over' and 'reduction to standard.'[2] Would we see the perceptually signalled objects themselves, seeing would be a simple matter—and it would be utterly confusing. For in each instance we would see what our eyes tell us, and they never tell us the same thing twice. But seeing (hearing, touching, etc.) is not a simple matter, and it is not (at least not usually) confusing. This is because we immediately refer our sensory information to our established *Gestalten* and it is these *Gestalten* that we apprehend clothed, as it were, in the sensuous material of actual perceptions. We see our sensory data *as* the familiar objects of our environing world, rather than seeing the data themselves. Seeing, as Hanson

---

[1] In Whitehead's language, we objectify our *data* (physical prehensions) with the forms of *eternal objects* (conceptual prehensions). Thus the P's are referred to, and are known in terms of, C's.

[2] Cf. the 'Appendix' below.

pointed out, is a 'theory-laden' (in the present view: *Gestalt*-laden) understanding.[1]

Our everyday world is populated with things and events which can be readily referred to invariant intelligible *Gestalten*. Indeed, we surround ourselves with things that we recognize, and tend to reduce that contingent of our experiential sphere which may be puzzling and unfamiliar. How this 'manipulation' of the environment to cognizable things may take place, is illustrated in the next diagram:

(21)

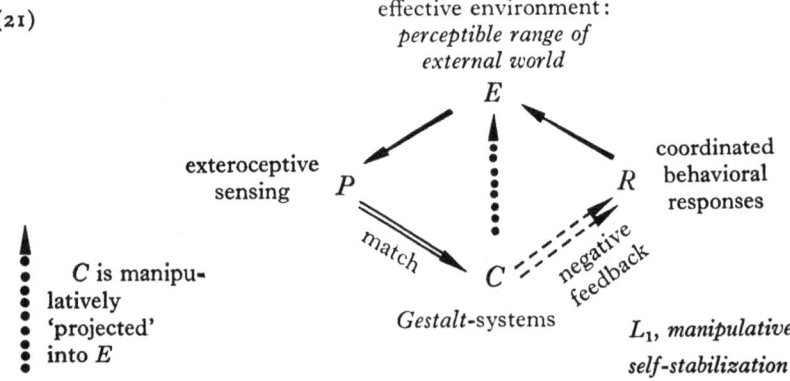

Behavioral responses (R) affect the environment—this is our impact as active and purposive beings on our surroundings. In this feedback activity we 'project our codes': shape and structure our environment with a view to bringing about perceptually cognizable things and events. (These are the kinds of things which are relevant to our needs, behavior patterns and projects.) Now, we inform ourselves of our environment through our exteroceptive senses. The latter give us perceptually cognizable information when the signals may be analyzed by, reduced or assimilated to, our *Gestalt*-systems. Our behavior is directed at the environment in function of providing us with sensory signals which remain invariant with respect to our already acquired elements of sensory knowledge. This relationship (represented by the double-shafted arrow) is assured by further behavioral responses directed at the perceptible environment in reference to our actual perceptions. And thus the manipulative cycle is set forth.

The manipulative cycle depends on the presence of intelligible C's for the interpretation of the sensory signals. The existing C's themselves must have been capable of being developed, however, and further ones must be able to develop if our P's are to be satisfactorily referred to them in the various phases and under the diverse conditions of our experience. We need

[1] N. R. Hanson, *Patterns of Discovery*, Cambridge, 1958, Chapter I.

a phase of feedback accounting for the phenomenon of *learning*. This is represented in the adaptive self-organization of the perceptual–cognitive circuit.

(22)

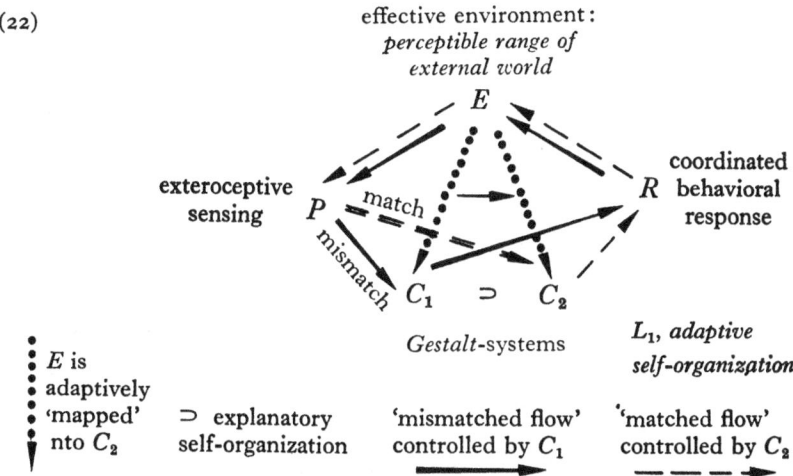

Learning, psychologists tell us, proceeds by the awareness of a problem, the setting up of hypotheses and trial and error activity testing the hypotheses. These elements are clearly present in the adaptive self-organization of the circuit. A single arrow connecting P to C_1 indicates that although P is referred to C, C is not invariant in regard to the former ('mismatch signal'). This represents a problem: the sensory signals are not cognized by means of an intelligible *Gestalt*. Various modes of fitting the sensory information to such *Gestalten* are essayed: the envisaged *Gestalten* represent the hypotheses ($C_2 \ldots C_n$). A new *Gestalt* can be confirmed by the trial and error process involving a behavioral response and the renewed perception of the effects. If the new *Gestalt* is confirmed, the perceptual–cognitive system accepts it as the proper representation of the given environmental state or object. That is, the new *Gestalt* (C_2) is mapped into the codes of the system and henceforth the system functions in reference to it, rather than to the previous *Gestalt* (C_1). In this view, learning signifies a reorganization of the cognitive system to accomodate the puzzling aspects of the received information. Such reorganization goes on constantly during all our waking hours and, it has been suggested, may even extend into the periods of sleep[1]. In our scheme the reorganization involves the replace-

[1] REM sleep may effect an integration of problematic experiences with those stored in memory, according to Louis Breger and his collaborators. Cf. *Time*, April 25, 1969.

ment of a 'mismatch signal' with a 'match signal' and the mapping of the code in virtue of which the match signal occurred. The process may continue over successive hypotheses until such a signal is obtained (i.e. until the sensory information is reduced to an intelligible *Gestalt*); or may stop when the puzzling information is forgotten or repressed and attention is redirected.

The adaptive function of the feedback system represents the processes of learning; the manipulative function those of acting on the environment to satisfy needs and wishes. Learning adapts the cognitive organism to the environment by evolving the codes which map its changing states within the nervous system, and manipulation adapts the environment to correspond to the existing codes of the organism. The outcome of these parallel (and in fact usually overlapping) operations is the constitution of a cognizable environment in which deliberate choices can be made with a view of maximising the assimilation of the 'external links' (such as food, mate, etc.) in the basic homeostatic feedback circuit of the organism. But, although the sensory cognitive circuit subserves the ends of the homeostatic one, it is not dependent for its completion on the latter. In consequence a total feedback pattern evolves which regulates and organizes experience in terms of the superordinate *Gestalt*-systems. In plain language, once we learn to know the world around us in terms of our sensory perceptions, we live as cognizing, rather than as instinctive and biochemically preprogramed beings. The instinctive genetically programed homeostatic activities continue, but are integrated into the total behavior pattern of the intelligent person, cognizant of his environment. And in this interpretation 'cognition of the environment' means that there are *Gestalten* for all major varieties of perceptible environmental states. The existing *Gestalten* are manipulatively projected into states of the environment, and unfamiliar environmental states, since no actual codes correspond to them, are adaptively mapped. Thus a significant level of information is extracted from our sense perceptions of the ever-changing environment.

III Meta-Sensory Feedback L_2 (Cultural Activities)

General Characteristics

Our hierarchy of information-flow levels contains three basic rungs: Levels L_0 (homeostasis), L_1 (perceptual cognition and behavior) and L_2. The last named constitutes the complex sphere of what I shall call, for want of a better name, 'cultural activity' on the *meta*-sensory level. (The

German word *Geist* as in '*Geisteswissenschaft*' comes closer to my intended meaning but its direct translation, 'spirit,' has misleading connotations.) The meta-sensory L_2 level includes such diverse areas of cognition and purposive behavior as science, art and religion. These, I shall argue, constitute the 'pure' modes of cultural activity, i.e. those which can be conceptually analyzed to distinct circuits of controlled information-flow. Such analysis does not imply that all cultural activities must be of the 'either-or' variety. In fact, mixed modes may ordinarily predominate. But clarity of exposition will prompt a separate treatment of the modes and their subsumption under conceptually distinct categories.

The explanation of the 'why' of culture poses serious problems. A plain sensory perception, cognition and correlated purposive behavior appears to be adequate to insure the survival of the individual and the species. Ordinary biological needs do not directly require cultural fulfillment. Must we assume then that some supra-biological (not to mention supra-natural) drive or force is operative in cultural man? I do not believe so. Culture may have biological adaptation value without being reducible to biology. It is possible to account for cultural modes of experience in consistent yet non-reductionist terms involving reference to basic system-activities, represented in information-flow charts. These activities may be hierarchically organized, although conserving an isomorphism of structure. The activity is directed at the extraction of increasingly higher levels of 'message' from 'noise,' i.e. at the discovery of further intelligible invariances in a fluctuating stream of information. Now, if ordinary perception has serious limitations as to its intelligibility, maintaining a correspondence between inputs and codes may motivate *meta*-perceptual cognitive processes. For, the input-code correspondence *must* be maintained. We know that all psychic functions occur in the framework of constant interaction between the nervous system and its environment. It is assumed that in the course of phylo- and ontogenesis statistical norms of interaction develop, and that any deviation from these norms produces a motivated activity tending to eliminate the differential. For example, sensory deprivation experiments show that there is a quantitative norm of sensory input which cannot be transgressed without entailing the serious malfunctioning of the entire nervous system.[1] The reduction of input below the norm produces disturbances which are intense and have considerable after-effects (i.e. the nervous system cannot immediately return to normal functioning when the input is again raised to the normal level). In addition to the quan-

---

[1] Cf. W. H. Bexton, W. Heron and T. H. Scott, 'Effects of Decreased Variation in the Sensory Environment' in *Canadian Journal of Psychology*, 1954, 8; also *Sensory Deprivation* (ed. P. Soloman), Cambridge, Mass. 1961, and pp. 97–98 below.

titative norms there appear to be qualitative, or informational norms as well. The sensory input must not only correspond to the norms of the nervous system quantitatively, but the input must also be patterned in a way which permits the nervous system to derive significant informations from it. For example, when an ape is brought up with eye-glasses which conduce light but prevent patterned visual perception, the animal becomes blind, exactly like one brought up in total darkness. The deprivation of the information content of perception has results similar to the deprivation of the quantity of the input: both result in the disorganization of the corresponding (and neglected) nervous functions.[1] Even a partial reduction of the information content of the input shows a marked correlation with reduction in higher nervous functions, e.g. in the case of animals whose visual or other perceptual field is significantly reduced and who develop a significantly lower level of intelligence than animals with normal input.

The motivation to reestablish norms takes precedence even over directly motivated activities, such as the satisfaction of hunger. Apes were observed to work for hours, opening doors, to find out what is going on outside; rats are known to first explore their new environment before satisfying their hunger, and so on. The reduction of the input in any respect—quantitative or qualitative—results in strong disturbances in the functioning of the central nervous system and the maintenance of the norms is, therefore, not surprisingly, a key factor in motivated activity.

The experimental findings referred to above permit the definition of the motivation which underlies purposive cognitive activity and experience. Motivation is defined as the a-specific drive to establish, and through feedback-stabilization maintain, the relation of transformation and invariance between the experiential input (proprioceptive and exteroceptive data, energies and substances) and the incorporated norms or codes (physiological as well as cognitive). Animal experiments show that the norms in question are those of certain quantities and qualities (patterns) of input. Other experiments, including those made on human subjects, show the distressing effects of any deprivation in the input. I conclude from the experimental data that the maintenance of a correspondence between the incorporated norms of the system and its interactive relations with the environment represents the precondition of the system's normal functioning and its basic motivation. This motivation is a-specific *qua* motivation, since it is triggered by any differential between the norms and the input. The motivation is reduced and ultimately may be (temporarily) eliminated by the activity resulting from it. This activity is specific, since it constitutes

[1] Cf. D. O. Hebb, *A Textbook of Psychology*, Philadelphia and London, 1958.

the purposive searching out of the discrepancy and the manipulative or adaptive activities required to reduce and eliminate it.

Thus motivation can trigger either one or both of the conceptually distinct but in fact interpenetrating processes which I denote 'manipulation' and 'adaptation.' Both processes have as their common goal the correspondence of input and norms but, whereas manipulation is directed toward bringing up the input to the level required for the code, adaptation is directed toward evolving the codes which fit the existing input. Hence both purposive environment-directed activity, and the various processes of learning, share the basic motivation of input-norm correspondence. The common motivation may be noted as $(P_1 \not\Rightarrow C) \rightarrow (P_2 \Rightarrow C)$ in the case of *manipulation*, where the activity is directed to produce the kind of P's to which an existent C will remain invariant; while motivation is noted $(P \not\Rightarrow C_1) \rightarrow (P \Rightarrow C_2)$ in the event of *learning*, where the activity is aimed at producing the C which will correspond, as an invariance, to given P's. The basic schema of motivation in cognitive activity is, in either case, $(P \not\Rightarrow C) \rightarrow (P \Rightarrow C)$. On the level of physiological homeostasis $(P \Rightarrow C)$ involves not much more than certain organic and kinesthetic stimuli and basic physiological norms. The former can constitute the system's normal input. But on the higher level of sensory-cognitive activity, the requirements imposed on the input by the codes are more stringent. They include, in addition to the stimuli signalling proper organic states, the sensory and perceptual patterns which provide the key to intelligibility in terms of sensory *Gestalten*. In other words, the input must not only satisfy the organic codes but also the system's norms of perceptual intelligibility.

In turning our attention to meta-sensory, i.e. *cultural* activities, such as those represented by the sciences, arts and religion, we must not search for activities directed at the intelligibility of the input in terms of perceived *Gestalten* alone, as in the case of perceptual–cognitive activity, for that would fail to distinguish these cultural fields from perceptual–cognitive activities manifested by most animals as well as men. Rather, we should consider the relationship between the more basic sensory circuits and the (assumedly) meta-sensory ones which would open the way for a consistent and yet non-reductionist linkage of ordinary cognitive circuits and the complex activity and experience patterns provided by cultural fields. The linkage can remain consistent, since the basic motivation, namely $(P \not\Rightarrow C) \rightarrow (P \Rightarrow C)$ is a-specific, permitting diverse types of specific activity patterns to evolve in its wake.

Now, the maintenance of the input-code correspondence (and therewith of an ongoing mapping of experienced states of the environment in the system) is sufficient to account for meta-perceptual—i.e. *cultural*—

cognition–patterns if, and only if, the sense–perceptual patterns prove to be inadequate in important respects. Such inadequacy led us to recognize the need for an environmentally cognizing feedback circuit when progressing from the level of the embryo to that of the developing infant and mature human being, and it is the one which now leads us to the consideration that the perceptual cognition of environmental events and entities is likewise insufficient for the purposes of modern man.

I shall reserve the predicate 'cultural' for self-stabilizing and self-organizing open systems whose cognitive requirements *exceed* the potentials of sense-codes. In other words, a cultural man is one who demands more information concerning his environment than he can obtain by means of assimilating his sensory input to sensory *Gestalten*. The latter fail him in two principal regards. First, they do not permit him to formulate deductively certain interrelations between his environmental events, thus making it impossible for him to predict their behavior with any semblance of certainty. Second, the familiar *Gestalten* of perceptual cognition fail to organize into a coherent and intelligible sequence the elements of *feeling* which permeate his apprehensions of his surroundings. Thus cultural man turns to modes of comprehension which transcend the realm of perceptual cognition. He undertakes 'cultural activities' in function of rendering his experience more intelligible. These activities operate on the level of autonomous circuits, stabilizing and organizing themselves isomorphically with the lower circuits. But their codes are not sensory but *meta-sensory* 'constructs,' 'intuitions,' 'visions,' and the like. Their development is motivated, consistently with the development of *Gestalt*-systems, by the manipulative and adaptive activities directed at $(P \not\Rightarrow C) \rightarrow (P \Rightarrow C)$. But the a-specific motivation is here forced into specific meta-sensory channels due to the failure of *Gestalt*-systems to satisfy the more stringent requirements of modern man. Hence specific varieties of meta-level feedback circuits are called into play, and these establish cognitive activity patterns which I shall identify as the experiential structures within which we develop our scientific theories, works of art and systems of religion.

Each of these L_2-level cultural cognitions and activities brings about a particular correlation between the codes of the system and the states of its environment. The codes are cognitive on these levels, rather than homeostatic physiological norms. But they are more than *sensory* cognitive codes, for they deal either with *relations* between *Gestalten* or the connoted *feelings* of the latter. In manipulatively as well as adaptively assuring the invariance of the system's codes with respect to its perceptual input, the circuits of cultural activity (science, art, religion and their various combinations) provide for a more accurate 'projection' of the system's codes into the environment, as well as for the precise 'mapping' of the states of the changing environment in the codes. The invariance of C with respect to P means that there is a code correlated with the state of the environment that is perceived. This environmental state is interpreted, in cultural circuits, not only in regard to its immediately perceptible qualities but also with respect to its theoretic and emotive implications and connotations. That is, cultural circuits derive a high level of information from the environment, producing further and more precise code/environmental state correlations than the lower circuits. We may thus say that cultural circuits bring about a more refined knowledge of the environment than either ordinary sense perception, or what Cannon so fittingly dubbed the 'wisdom of the body.'

Specific Meta-Sensory Circuits

(a) Meta-Sensory Feedback L_{21} (Scientific Activity)

The world of perceptual–cognitive activity depends for its intelligibility on *Gestalt*-systems. The thus disclosed world is the world of the radical empiricist; it is a world where no departure from the immediately given experience appears to take place (since the P's are 'seen *as*' the C's rather than consciously interpreted in terms of the latter). But this world suffers serious limitations in regard to its intelligibility. Sensory objects pass in review therein, like actors on a stage (to use Hume's imaginative simile) and there is no way to establish necessary connections between them. Hence we can neither predict the events of our experience nor reason to events beyond those which we actually apprehend. To do either of these things we must make inferences of a kind which transcend the sensory realm of the radical empiricist. If we are of his sceptical temper, we shall desist, and restrict ourselves to the sensory realm of immediate experience. But if we share some of the suppositions of the rationalist, we shall bring the empiricism of the sceptic in conjunction with the trust in reason of the rationalist and penetrate into the partly rationalistic realm of science. In this realm, which is that of system-theory, we can undertake an investigation of meta-sensory reality, on condition that we test our conclusions against experience.

The particular meta-sensory domain of science is based on the use of rational 'constructs.' Such a construct endows the elements of experience with logical coherence. It enables one to reason about these elements with deductive cogency. It makes conceptual manipulation of the elements possible, beyond the observation of the merely incidental correlations which Hume has shown to prevail among our perceptions. The principle of causality, for example, cannot be perceived, nor can it be derived from perceptions. It must be rationally 'constructed.' Among perceptions, regularities reduce to accidental orderings. Logical necessity and coherence must be introduced by reason, rather than be abstracted from experience. Hence rational construction is forced upon all people who are dissatisfied with the incidental connections of sensory *Gestalten* and who wish to obtain deductive proof of their correlation. Rational construction places the experienced items in definite connection with causal, mathematical and similar 'operators,' and subjects thereby the data to precise manipulation—ultimately to prediction and control. The inquiring mind is thus forced to turn to a meta-level code in precisely interpreting its perception, and this meta-level code will be a 'rational construct'; an entity of science.

The gradual historical evolution of scientific thought testifies to the painstaking development of such a meta-circuit of cognitive activity. In the history of science the overall trend has been to proceed from the organization of sensory *Gestalten*, and classes of such *Gestalten* (such as fire, water, air and earth) to an abandonment of these *Gestalten* in favor of empirical–rationalistically constructed events and entities. Thereby the naïve realist sensory world, which fathered science, has been consumed by its own offspring. 'Naïve realism' said Russell, 'leads to physics, and physics, if true, shows that naïve realism is false. Therefore naïve realism, if true, is false; therefore it is false.'[1]

To analyse the gradual breakdown of the naïvely realist sensory world would require a separate volume. I may note, however, that the outcome of the historical evolution of science is that our reified subject–predicate constituted *Gestalt*-systems are all but exploded and replaced by scientific constructs. Contemporary empirical sciences aspire to the state of physics, which consists of a large superstructure of constructs interrelated by means of 'rules of correspondence' (or 'epistemic correlations') with highly specific sensory data. The selection of the latter is operational, being dictated by their relevance to all components in the field of constructs. Constructs, systematically connected in a theory, generate predictions as to the occurrence of certain sensory data. Their actual occurrence or non-occurrence decides the validity of the system of constructs.

I shall not deal here with the numerous criteria for selecting the constructs,[2] but merely note that the constructs are not sense-perceived

---

[1] Bertrand Russell, *An Inquiry into Meaning and Truth*, Harmondsworth, 1962, p. 13.

[2] Cf. for example, the 'Metaphysical Requirements on Constructs' in Henry Margenau, *The Nature of Physical Reality*, New York 1950, Chapter 5.

Levels of Controlled Information-flow in Experience

Gestalten but rational constructions, designed to exhibit the interconnection of the perceived items of experience deductively, from axiomatic premisses. The sum of confirmed constructs is taken to be a conceptual representation of the nature of reality; a reality which is the 'effective environment' of science: the 'natural universe.'

The general information flow of scientific theory formulation and testing may be charted as follows:

(23)

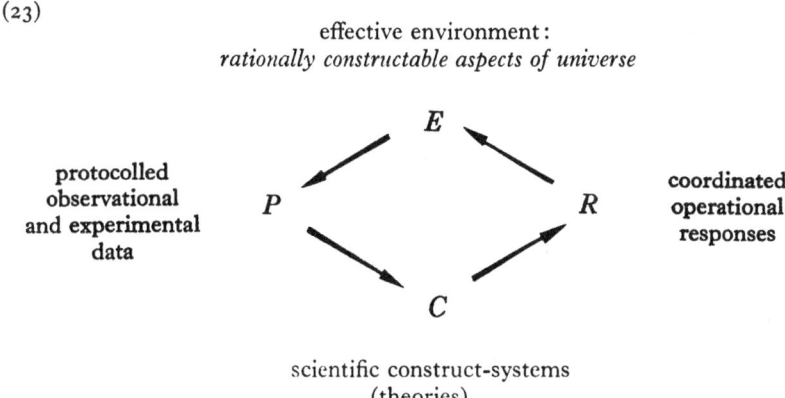

effective environment:
rationally constructable aspects of universe

protocolled observational and experimental data — P

coordinated operational responses — R

scientific construct-systems
(theories)

L_{21}, *general information-flow*

Observation in science represents a passage from highly selected items of observational and experimental evidence to a system of constructs making up a theory. The passage here is not determined by ordinary ways of regarding the world and acting in relation to it, but by the sum of scientific knowledge at one's disposal. The *P*'s are not assimilated to a familiar sensory *Gestalt*, i.e. they are not seen *as* such a familiar entity, but are referred beyond themselves to constructs, some of which can be observationally tested and many of which cannot, otherwise than by passing through the testable constructs. Thus 'wavelength' associated with the perception of a red light can be observationally confirmed by adjusting the spectroscope, whereas no amount of experiment can produce observational evidence for an electron or its ψ-function. The latter type of construct can only be indirectly tested, in reference to the observational evidence for constructs with which it is systematically interrelated within the theory.[1]

---

[1] Examples of observationally testable, i.e. 'epistemically connected' constructs are given by the relation between a force and an awareness of muscular exertion; the weight of an object and a reading on a scale, a wavelength and the discernment of a line on a photographic plate. Examples of indirectly testable, i.e. 'formally

The appropriate expression characterizing the passage from data to construct is not seeing *as*, but seeing *that* . . . The 'that' refers to the unseen and perhaps unseeable construct which the scientist associates with his observations. Thus the physicist can see *that* a field of a given strength is associated with his observational objects, although field-strength itself is not an observable. The majority of scientific constructs comes into this category, beginning with the constructs 'mass,' 'energy,' 'light' and 'causality' and progressing to the highly abstract notions of space-time invariance, and nucleonic, electronic, gravitational and electromagnetic fields.

The importance and ubiquity of such constructs is best illustrated by cases when they are not present. Hanson describes such cases, where the observational data are not referred to existing constructs. 'In microscopy one often reports sensations in a phenomenal, lustreless way: "it is green in this light; darkened areas mark the broad end . . ." So too the physicist may say: "the needle oscillates, and there is a faint streak near the neon parabola. Scintillations appear on the periphery of the cathodescope . . .".' However, these cases are, Hanson tells us, overstressed. They apply to the experimental situation, where confusion and even conceptual muddle may dominate. They do not apply to situations where scientific *knowledge* is brought to bear. 'Every physicist forced to observe his data as in an oculist's office finds himself in a special, unusual situation. He is obliged to forget what he knows and to watch events like a child.'[1] What, then, applies to the situation involving scientific *knowledge*, i.e. applicable, or at least relevant, constructs (*C*'s)? Hanson gives the following example.

'To see [in a representation] an X-ray tube is to see that a photo-sensitive plate below it will be irradiated. It is to see that the target will be extremely hot, and as it has no water jacket it must be made of metal with a high melting-point—molybdenum or tungsten. It is to see that at high voltages green fluorescence will appear at the anode.' The photo-sensitive plate, its irradiation, the temperature of the target, the type of metal it is made of, high voltages and fluorescence are not seen 'in' the representation of an X-ray tube—they are seen *in virtue of it*—always provided that the

---

connected' constructs are all relations between geometric quantities which are provable on the basis of a suitable set of axioms; the relation between force and the acceleration of a given mass (Newton's laws); between a point charge and its electromagnetic field (Maxwell's equations); between the temperature of a molecule and the mean kinetic energy of a gas (Gibbs' statistical mechanics); and between the curvature of space and the quantity of matter in that region (Einstein's general relativity). Cf. Margenau, *op. cit.* pp. 84ff.

[1] Hanson, *op. cit.*, p. 20.

things here enumerated are already known, i.e. that 'X-ray tube' is a meaningful proposition. 'A child could parrot X-ray tube...' says Hanson, 'when confronted with the figure above, but he would not see that these other things followed. And this is what the physicist does see.'[1]

Hence in science 'seeing' is 'seeing *that*' in reference to scientific C's. 'Observation is physics (Hanson points out) is not an encounter with unfamiliar and unconnected flashes, sounds, and bumps, but rather a calculated meeting with these flashes, sounds and bumps of a particular kind—this might figure as an account of what observation is.' And this statement applies, naturally, not only to physics but to all empirical sciences. It is precisely by referring the 'flashes, sounds and bumps' to a set of rigorously constructed and connected C's that scientific knowledge becomes possible. The flashes, etc., are meaningless in themselves; what lends them meaning is their epistemic correlation with the C's.

So far I have discussed science's passage from P to C. This is the purely cognitive aspect of the scientific endeavor, and treatments of scientific method often end there. But I suggest that, in order to see the full picture, we must also inquire into the passage from C to R and from R to E and back again to P. That is, we must trace out the full feedback cycle if we are to give an adequate account of the structure of scientific activity.

I shall not contend that scientific theories are formulated *in order that* particular responses could be made to them. That would be to disregard the cognitive aim of pure science and to unduly emphasize one of the terms involved in the feedback circuit. However, one may affirm that, after the purely cognitive phase, of referring P's to C's, a passage to R does take place. It does, already because the cognitive aim of science can only be accomplished through the process of confirming the hypotheses, which is a feedback circuit involving coordinated response by the scientist on his test object, and his perception of the resulting state of the object. (The operational emphasis can be replaced by successive observations, where the time interval represents the 'manipulation' of the test-object, and the perceived difference in the state of the object measured by a temporal scale indicates confirmation or falsification.) Such theories often prove amenable to application, whereby controlled processes are initiated, which restructure some part of the experience of the scientist—and eventually of everyone in his society. The circuit is completed in all these instances.

The rational–empirically coded feedback circuit typical of contemporary science may be subdivided, similarly to the perceptual–cognitive circuit, into a manipulative and an adaptive system (fig. 24).

[1] *Ibid.*, pp. 22–23.

(24)

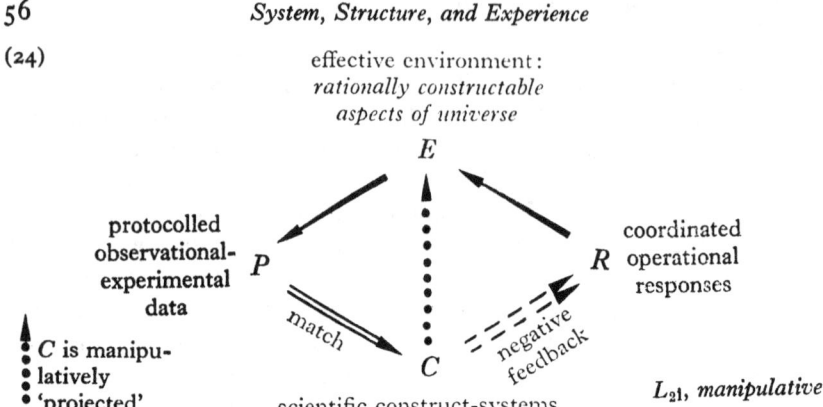

The functions of the self-stabilizing feedback circuit of the scientific circuit of cognition and operational response may be read off the graph. The operational responses of the scientist (or technician) modify the relevant states of the environment. The modifications are perceived and are correlated with operations in function of reducing the margin of error with the constructs. Hence the operations bring about states in the environment which confirm the constructs: these states can be 'seen *that*' the postulated scientific entities (or laws) are in effect. The scientist can be said to 'project his constructs' into the environment if by that we do not mean that he actually makes his postulates appear in his surroundings, but only that he brings about perceptions which are correlated by his postulated rules of correspondence with his constructs. This is not to suggest that he can confirm any construct. The test of empirical confirmation decides the validity of his scheme: it decides which of his constructs are 'projectable,' i.e. which of them find exemplification as actualities in the natural universe.

Now, the manipulative self-stabilization of the scientific verification-process is constantly corrected and supplemented by its adaptive self-organization. The latter's information-flow is charted in figure (25). The scheme gives the dynamics of theory-formulation—the scientific variant of the process of 'learning.' The single arrow connecting P to C_1 indicates that the protocol data are not interpretable as transformations of invariant laws (or other constructs). This poses the problem toward the resolution of which various hypotheses are advanced ($C_1 \ldots C_2$). These require testing, and that means passing through $R \rightarrow E \rightarrow P$. A successful hypothesis is one which is confirmed by accomodating the hitherto puzzling P's as transformations of an invariant construct (C_2). In Margenau's terminology, these C's then become *verifacts*. They are assigned existential reality and are viewed, as the sense-codes were, as cognitions of states of E.

(25)

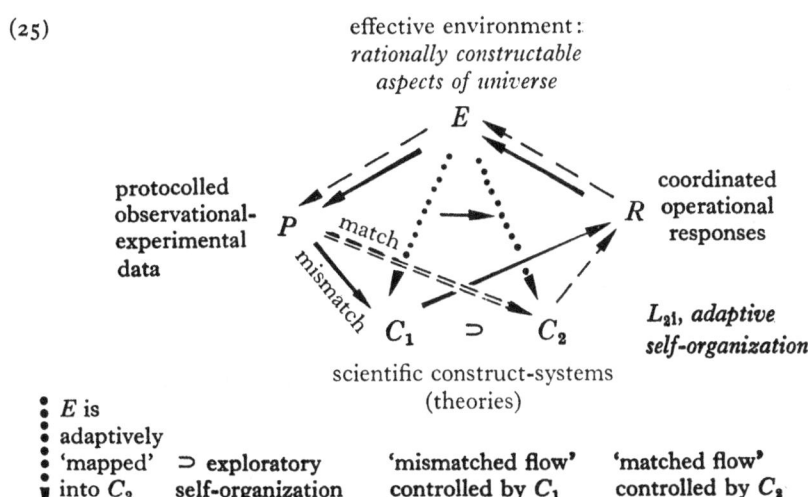

The E in question is extended considerably beyond the realm of perceptual cognition: it is now the 'natural universe' (this term indicates the environment to which science makes reference; it does not carry warranty that it is the 'real' world discussed by speculative metaphysicians). It is this universe which is adaptively mapped in the constantly evolving self-corrective construct–systems of science.

(b) Meta-Sensory Feedback L_{211} (Aesthetic Activity)

My remarks concerning the insufficiency of *Gestalt*-systems to elucidate cultural man's experience assigned specific values both to science and to art. As regards science, there is agreement at least as to the specificity and fundamental unity of all instances of scientific activity. There is some understanding concerning what constitutes a scientific entity. But aesthetics is a controversial field, where little agreement as to what constitutes an 'aesthetic phenomenon' is reached. Some aestheticians have questioned whether such an agreement *can* be reached, even in regard to works of art. Morris Weitz points out that 'Even if art has one set of necessary and sufficient properties, ... no aesthetic theory yet proposed has enumerated that set to the satisfaction of all concerned.'[1] His understanding of aesthetic theory is 'not to conceive it as definition, logically doomed to failure, but to read it as summaries of seriously made recommendations to attend certain ways to certain features of art.' However, the difficulty with his conclusion is that it begs the question. 'How can we determine

[1] Morris Weitz, 'The Role of Theory in Aesthetics,' *The Journal of Aesthetics and Art Criticism*, Vol. XV, No. 1.

what is excellent in art' asked Erich Kahler in his reply to Weitz, 'as long as we have not established a clear notion of the distinct character of art?'[1] It would seem more indicated, therefore, to approach the original assumption, that the definition of art is 'logically doomed to failure,' in a more positive spirit: it may be that failure is due to the limited insight of individual aestheticians, and not to the prohibitive nature of the subject matter itself. We might take aesthetic theories as working hypotheses, even if we reject them as confirmed theories. Then we could explore their applicability to aesthetic phenomena, especially art. Whether or not any existing aesthetics has furnished us with a list of the necessary and sufficient conditions of aesthetic things and events does not preclude that such conditions be definable. It may well be, moreover, that the scrutiny of existing theories may lead to further insights leading toward their definition.

I shall approach the field of aesthetics in this positive but non-dogmatic spirit. On so doing I can note a consensus of views as regards specific aspects of art, and aesthetic phenomena in general. The first and perhaps most basic of these is that art, and aesthetics in general, is concerned with the intuition and appreciation of sensuous materials, i.e. with the immanent contents of sensory perception, rather than with its transcendent signification. This view, subscribed to by such men as Roger Fry, Benedetto Croce, R. G. Collingwood and innumerable others, has been most succinctly put by Northrop. 'The distinguishing mark [of art] is that its *primary* concern is with immediately experienced materials. The painter does not talk about colors, after the manner of the mathematical physicist; he puts before one the directly sensed particular blue, red, yellow, etc., each instance of any one being unique, as are their similar seen shapes. Conversely, the primary concern of the mathematical physicist is to use the impressionistic painter's emotively moving immediately apprehended colors, not in and for themselves, but merely instrumentally as the means for inferring, and the data for confirming or disconfirming, the quite different invariant mathematical laws of electromagnetic propagations both within the so-called visible portion, and the many different non-visible segment, of the spectrum of electromagnetic possibilities.'[2]

The point made by Northrop is of capital importance for aesthetics; it concerns the immediacy of its passage from P to C. It is also made by Benedetto Croce: '. . . the red in a painted face does not there represent the red color of the physicists, but is a characteristic element of the portrait.

---

[1] Erich Kahler, 'What is Art?' in *Problems of Aesthetics* (ed. Weitz), New York, 1959.

[2] F. S. C. Northrop, 'Toward a General Theory of the Arts,' *The Journal of Value Inquiry*, Vol. I, No. 2.

The whole is that which determines the quality of the parts. A work of art may be full of philosophical concepts; it may contain them in greater abundance and they may there be even more profound than in a philosophical dissertation, which in turn may be rich to overflowing with descriptions and intuitions. But notwithstanding all these concepts the total effect of the work of art is an intuition and notwithstanding all those intuitions, the total effect of the philosophical dissertation is a concept[1].' Abstracting from the Cocean definition of 'intuition,' we may simply note that it is contrasted with 'concept' in the same way that Northrop's 'emotively moving immediately apprehended colors' are contrasted with the instrumental means to which the physicist puts colors, in inferring and confirming his invariant scientific laws. Absorption in the immediacy of perception is generally recognized as the characteristic mark of art, whereas the instrumental use of perceptions to infer and confirm theories is the typical mark of science. Let me ask, then: what is it in his sensory experience which absorbs the artist as well as the art lover? Are we talking of the same P's which were 'seen *as*' *Gestalten* and 'seen *that*' they imply scientific constructs?

The P's in question are those which are delivered by our exteroceptive senses: they are therefore the same as the protocol data of science and the elements constituting sensory *Gestalten*. The perceived color red is a P, and it is shared by our sensory cognition of a face seen in real life, by our aesthetic appreciation of a painted face on a canvas, and by a red light in the laboratory of the mathematical physicist. But its mode of treatment differs radically. The same color red may be 'seen *as*' the face of a woman in the street, 'seen *that*' it is of a certain wavelength of radiation, and it may also be, I submit, '*felt as*' a particularly lucid and aesthetically satisfying emotion.

The assumption, that immediate sensory experience is infused with emotional coloring, has hitherto been made only by thinkers who have not hesitated to deal with emotion, rather than relegating it to the limbo of philosophically meaningless phenomena. Perhaps the most remarkable of these was Whitehead who told us that 'the separation of the emotional experience from the primitive presentational intuition is a high abstraction of thought.'[2] In his view primitive experience is infused with the emotional coloring of aversion and adversion. This insight is now corroborated by findings in the field of experimental neurophysiology. Basing his views on carefully controlled experiments, Grastyán states that the basic attitude of

[1] Benedetto Croce, 'Art as Intuition' from *Aesthetic*, reprinted in *Problems of Aesthetics, op. cit.*
[2] A. N. Whitehead, *Process and Reality*, New York 1929, p. 247.

the nervous system in regard to a given object is one of attraction or repulsion.[1] The theory finds support in the experimental findings of Olds and his collaborators, who found that the cortexes of rats can be stimulated through electrodes, both so that the rats are attracted by the stimulation and so that they are repulsed by it.[2] The two effects were subsequently found to be confined to determinate areas in the nervous system. With this an objective basis of measurement was given to hitherto subjectively and primarily introspectively known emotional experiences.

If we agree with Grastyán, that the basic attitude of the system toward given objects includes the emotional elements of attraction or repulsion, we find that adversive and aversive emotions are indeed, as Whitehead told us, an intimate part of primitive experience. ('Thus the primitive experience is emotional feelings, felt in its relevance to a world beyond.') An entire continuum of wide range of emotional coloring may be given by the direction and intensity of the basic *pro* or *contra* attitudes. Both directions may have various levels of intensity, with the result that the full scale of feelings may be embraced by the hypothesis, ranging from unqualified and intense repulsion to similarly unqualified and intense attraction.[3]

The linear schema of emotional qualities would require to be modified, however, in the light of experimental evidence which shows that the test animals find the same type of stimulation pleasant at relatively weak levels of intensity and unpleasant at higher levels.[4] Thus just when something is felt to be pleasant (feeling of attraction) and unpleasant (repulsion) needs to be determined in reference to specific physiological and nervous norms, rather than in exclusive reference to the object or stimulation itself. The precise determination of these conditions can be left to experimental neurophysiology; for our purposes I may merely conclude that certain elements of our sensory input may be infused with varying shades of attractive or repulsive ('pull' and 'push') emotions. While one and the

[1] E. Grastyán, 'Utban az emberi emóciók megértése felé' (On the Way to the Understanding of Human Emotions') in *Valóság*, Budapest, 1968, 6.

[2] J. Olds and P. Milner, 'Positive Reinforcement Produced by Electrical Stimulation of Septal Area and Other Regions of Rat Brain' in *Journal of Comparative Psychology*, XLVII (1954).

[3] The above empirical conclusion was fully anticipated by Whitehead: 'Anger, hatred, fear, terror, attraction, love, hunger, eagerness, massive enjoyment, are feelings and emotions closely entwined with the primitive functioning of 'retreat from' and of 'expansion towards.' They arise in the higher organism as states due to a vivid apprehension that some such primitive mode of functioning is dominating the organism.' *Symbolism, Its Meaning and Effect, op. cit.*, p. 45.

[4] E. Grastyán, G. Karmos, L. Vereczkey, J. Martin and L. Kellényi, 'Hypothalamic Motivational Processes as Reflected by their Hippocampal Electrical Correlates' in *Science*, CXLIX (1965).

same type of input may, under changing circumstances, change sign from attraction to repulsion, or vice versa, it is a reasonable generalization that certain kinds of stimulations tend, under most circumstances, to be felt as pleasant, respectively as unpleasant. And if so, then we may assume that the typical emotional charge of the given type of input becomes associated with it through a process of emotional 'imprinting' with the result that whenever the datum recurs, its typical associated emotional charge tends to accompany it. Hence flowers, clean air, the smell of hay are typically pleasant (attractive) olfactory stimulants, while ordure and garbage are the opposite. Similar examples can be readily found for visual, auditory, tactile and gustatory stimulation, as well as for organic and kinesthetic sensations. I may conclude, then, that our ordinary experience of ourself and the world is infused with many shades of adversive and aversive emotions, typically associated in most cases with recurrent types of stimulation. This entire world of feeling and emotion is part and parcel of human (as well as animal) experience, and if the purely factual aspect of experience needs to be organized to recurrent invariances, so does this part. Thus the basic a-specific motivation $(P \not\Rightarrow C) \rightarrow (P \Rightarrow C)$ may result in specific activity patterns in regard both to the *factually informative*, as well as to the *emotive* aspect of the input.

Now, science, while it is the activity circuit *par excellence* of factually evaluated sensory inputs, is almost totally incompetent to deal with the emotive aspect of the data. The emotive aspect of human experience is not organized by scientific theories, no matter how successful they may be in their own fields. The Rock of Gibraltar may be scientifically analyzed to the erosive action of sea and wind through the eons of the earth's evolution, but this will not prevent the scientist from apprehending it as a majestic mountain rising from the sea. Science may analyze a human being to a system of homeostatically regulated molecules, cells and organs, the scientist cannot help but continue to be inspired by feelings of love, friendship, sympathy or aversion. Since immediate experience is infused with feeling, and neither our *Gestalt*-systems nor the rational constructs of science can adequately organize them to intelligibility and meaningfulness, a meta-level circuit other than science needs to be evolved.[1] I suggest that this circuit of activity constitutes art and the general realm of aesthetic enjoyment and activity. Its general information-flow can be represented as follows:

---

[1] This is not to contest that science can and does investigate the neural and behavioral coordinates of feelings. Yet the particular 'mismatch' that occurs when a person finds his *felt* experience unintelligible is not removed by the statement of a neurological or psychological theory, no matter how accomplished these may be.

(26)

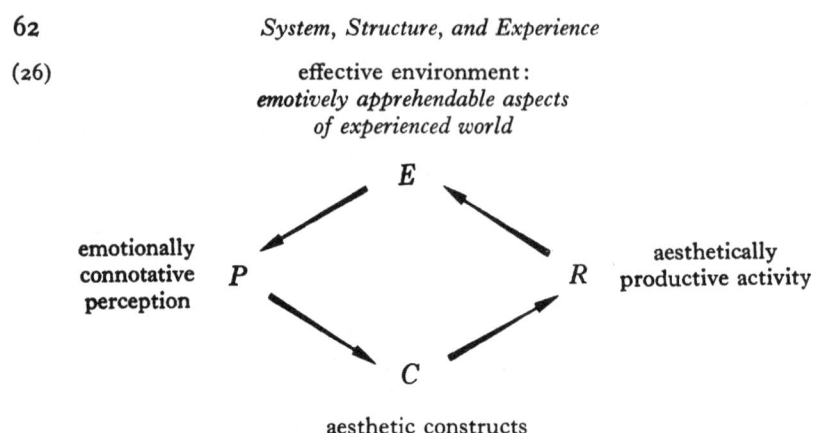

L_{211}, *general information-flow*

To perceive the emotively moving sensory materials displayed for us by the artist and thereby to organize and clarify our inchoate feelings, thus discovering them in consciousness, has been said to be the principal function of art by Collingwood. In somewhat different contexts, the essentially emotive (i.e. not 'meaningless' but 'non-factually significant') nature of art has been affirmed by a host of writers on aesthetics. Many, if not most of them would subscribe to the basic proposition, that an aesthetic experience involves beholding a sensory pattern and thereby obtaining a lucid and satisfying, typically aesthetic emotion. I could restate this proposition to read—We interpret[1] our emotively charged P's in terms of invariant aesthetic constructs, i.e. C's representing the lucid and satisfying aesthetic emotions. The aesthetic experience obtains if, and only if, our P's are interpretable in terms of the C's. It should not be possible to obtain such an experience in the absence of P's (except by *imagining* the appropriate P's, in which case they are present to our minds, if not through sensory stimulation, then through vivid recollection). This is consistent with the consensus of opinion which designates an absorption in sensory elements as an essential condition of aesthetic experience. It should also not be possible to obtain an aesthetic experience in the absence of C's in terms of which the given (or imagined) P's could be interpreted, since the C's guarantee the hallmark of aesthetic experience: clarified and satisfactory feeling. This is consistent with the consensus of opinion, based on

---

[1] In the context of aesthetics, 'interpret' does not mean a conceptual process. It denotes a spontaneous discovery of emotive significance, a non-conceptual (but for all that no less meaningful) passage from P to C. Cf. p. 68n.

solid observational evidence, that the appreciation of any work of art, or instance of natural beauty, is directly conditioned by one's previous acquaintance with that style, or that kind of scenery, i.e. by one's having *learned* to appreciate it. Here we must be careful to distinguish between 'clarified and satisfying feeling' and a plain sense of amazement, such as something entirely new might inspire. A peasant from Outer Mongolia may be conscious of amazement, and perhaps even of a delightful sense of surprise, on hearing Richard Strauss' *Till Eulenspiegel*; he will not be likely, however, to find that it inspires lucid and satisfying emotions in him. Conversely, the typical Western music lover, exposed to traditional Oriental music, will perhaps be amazed at the drumming and wailing he hears, but will not find it significant, in the way the Oriental exposed to such music presumably finds it. Hence *both* the P's and the C's are required for an aesthetic experience, and the P's must be interpretable by the C's. To enjoy a symphony we must perceive musical sounds and find them significant—and not every set of musical sounds is a symphony, and not every symphony is found aesthetically significant. The same applies, *mutatis mutandis*, to colors, shapes, words and the various arts which make use of them.

This position suggests that aesthetic constructs have been established in our minds through cultural and stylistic habituation. Whenever our sensory experiences correspond to these, be they instances of art or of natural scenery, we interpret them accordingly. In art we do not pass to C's *beyond* our sensory experience, as we do in science, where they are reached by means of inference governed by rules of correspondence, but to *immanent* C's, rather like *Gestalten*, which let us interpret the P's in a meaningful manner. Aesthetic constructs represent 'visions' or 'intuitions'; having them means a capacity to enjoy aesthetic sensations if and when presented with the appropriate scenes and objects (and perhaps even when imaginatively recalling them). We enjoy our C's when we interpret P's in their terms. That is, we discover patterns of colors, surfaces, sequences of sounds or actions, as emotively significant, lucid and satisfying. The process is essentially analogous to other passages from P to C: the P's are interpreted as examples ('transformations') of C. We cognize by *recognizing*: we discover that the lucid and satisfactory emotions which we already know from past experience can be 'expressed' in these particular phases.

That this discovery gives the true meaning of 'expression' in art is also evident from Herbert Read's notion of the three stages of artistic appreciation. The first stage, he tells us, consists of the mere perception of material qualities (sounds, colors, etc.), and the second of the arrangement of these qualities into particular shapes and patterns. The third stage comes 'when such an arrangement of perceptions is made to correspond with a previously existing state of emotion or feeling. Then we say that the emotion or feeling is given *expression*.'[1] That this correspondence can be read as the transformations (by the patterns of perception) of an invariance in feeling is evident from Read's assertion: 'The permanent element in mankind that corresponds to the element of form in art is man's aesthetic sensibility. It is the sensibility that is static. What is variable is the interpretation which man gives to the forms of art, which are said to be 'expressive' when they correspond to his immediate feelings.' The matching of variable interpretations of forms to static sensibilities can be stated as the passage from variable P's to invariant *immanent* C's. Since the key element is emotive quality, we can state this passage (by adapting Hanson's terminology) as a 'feeling *as*.' We *feel* the perceived materials of the artist's work *as* evoking in us clear and satisfying feelings; we so feel the sounds of a Symphony and the words and events of a play. It matters not that we also conceptualize (if and when we do) our experience of the work and glean ideas from it as well as feelings. The ideas gleaned from a play relate to our total experience of it as elements of the emotions the play as a whole evokes in us. Even if we 'see Hamlet *as*' a tragic human being, and even if we 'see *that*' he is avenging a wrong, the play as a whole we 'feel *as*' significant.

Positivistic thinkers tend to reduce cognitive experience to science. For them we must see, and cannot *feel* significantly. I take issue with this dogma (for that is what I believe it to be) and subsume aesthetic activity under the circuits of *cognitive* activities. The reason for this lies with my interpretation of 'significance.' If we hold that a *seen P*, if it coincides with an entertained C as its transformation, gives us an example of cognition, we must by the same token hold that a *felt P*, if it thus satisfies an invariant C, provides us with cognition. For we map our P's by C's and interpret them in terms of the latter, and it matters little whether the nature of the passage is conceptual or non-conceptual. *Cognition occurs whenever the P's satisfy the C's.* But the *contents* of cognition, of course, will be strongly affected. The contents are sensory data and their epistemically correlated scientific or otherwise postulated rationalistic constructs in the case of *seen P*'s, and they are feelings in the case of *felt P*'s. But is not a knowledge about feeling valid knowledge? If our experience consists not only of cut-and-dried 'sense-data' but also of moving, spontaneous and ineffable elements of sensation, is not truth about the latter still truth? Collingwood told us that art is knowledge: it is knowledge of one's immediate, non-intellectually elaborated experience. Such experience is not as yet subdivided by the intellect into an 'I' and a 'world.' A knowledge of it is not a

---

[1] Sir Herbert Read, *The Meaning of Art*, London, 1931.

knowledge of the self, nor of the not-self, but of both—a knowledge of how it feels to exist, to perceive, to act. Commonsense and science transmutes these elements of experience into quantitative, rational facts, or disregards them altogether. Art crystallizes them into conscious, lucid emotion, into a knowledge of feeling. It is this interpretation that I propose of 'significance' in the context of aesthetics. It is the counterpart of 'knowledge' in ordinary perceptual cognitive activity and its rationalistically extended and confirmed form in science. The synaesthetic unity of primitive experience is surrendered in cultural cognition: the rationally constructable aspects cohere into science and the emotively apprehendable facets crystallize into art.

Let us next consider the nature of the passage from such 'significant' (i.e. lucid, satisfying, 'truthful') feelings to the *responses* to them. The symbol R denotes, in the context of aesthetic activity, all purposive responses to aesthetic experiences. It is not restricted to artistic creativity, but finds adequate exemplification in interpretation and appreciation as well. The function of R is, in all cases, to bring about perceptions which function as particular transformations of our significant and satisfying feelings. In other words, its function is a cognitive one, despite the emotive nature of the perceptions.[1] I am speaking of manipulative self-stabilization, the information-flow of which may be represented in the following chart:

(27)
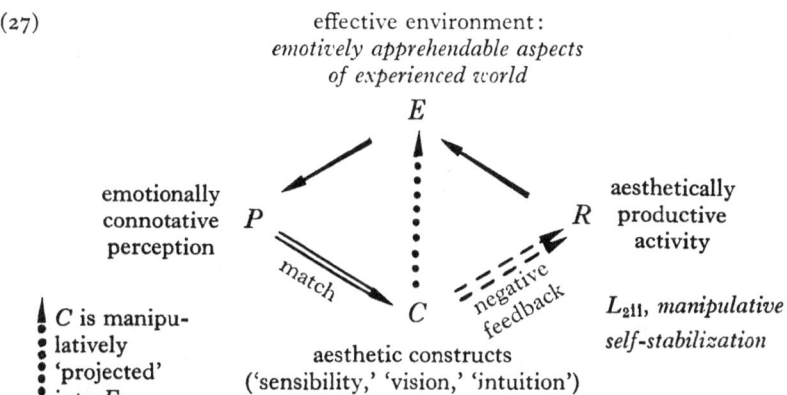

[1] Many writers (e.g. Fry, Parker, Croce, Bullough Cassirer) emphasize that art produces, or requires, no response of a practical kind. But no writer would readily deny, I believe, that there is a response to art and that this response is directed at the continued attainment, or maximization, of the aesthetic experience. Thus the issue is not whether or not there is an active response to art, but whether the response is confined to the sphere of the aesthetic experience or transcends it. I maintain the former: the objective of the response is the attainment and stabilizaton of the experience around the aesthetic standards of the person.

The artist (interpreter, appreciator) manipulates his environment so as to make his perceptions of it conform to his aesthetic sensibilities. He 'projects' his aesthetic vision into environmental 'control objects.' His 'aesthetic vision' corresponds, notwithstanding differences of detail between the individual doctrines, to Croce's 'intuition,' Cassirer's 'dynamic form,' Fry's 'order and variety in the imaginative life,' Collingwood's 'total activity apprehended by the use of imagination,' as well as to Pepper's 'satisfaction in felt quality.'[1] It matters little whether C is possessed in fullness and clarity before R is initiated or whether engaging in R actually helps clarify C through trial-and-error testing. Croce would maintain that C ('intuition') is prior to the creation of the physical artifact which, in his view, is merely metaphorically called 'work of art.' Creating the artifact has nothing to do with art itself; only with communication. Intuition—which is held to be the same as expression (a proper intuition is implicitly expressed, at least for oneself) is 'art.' That is, for Croce art *is* C, irregardless of R. R (the aesthetic activity) comes in only as a technique of communicating *my* C to *you*. Cassirer, on the other hand, for whom C is 'dynamic form,' maintains that '... for a great painter, a great musician, or a great poet, the colors, the lines, rhythms, and words are not merely part of his technical apparatus; they are necessary moments of the productive process itself.'[2] Similarly Collingwood, who defines C as lucid and satisfying emotion, objects to the view that the artist fully knows what he is about before he sets out to do it. 'The artist proper is a person who, grappling with the problem of expressing a certain emotion, says, "I want to get this clear".'[3] This controversy traverses the field of contemporary aesthetic theory and thus deserves mention. It is without ultimate importance for this theory, however, since whether there is a trial-and-error feedback during the creative process which shapes C, or whether C is complete in all essentials and the creative process serves merely to project and externalize it, aesthetic activity remains one which shapes the perceptible environment so that the artist's sensory experience is made to conform to his vision. This is merely to paraphrase the proposition, that R is directed toward E in function of reducing P to a transformation of C. Whether the invariance is assured purely through the manipulative phase of the feedback cycle, or also involves the adaptive one (cf. below), is without

---

[1] The author is most grateful to Professor Pepper for pointing this out to him. The many, and for him most heartening, points of agreement between this self-stabilizing self-organizing system and Pepper's 'selective system' deserve to be explored in more detail. Cf. Stephen C. Pepper, *Concept and Quality*, La Salle, Ill. 1966.

[2] Ernst Cassirer, *An Essay on Man*, New Haven, 1944.

[3] Collingwood, *op. cit.*

major importance. It is quite probable that this varies from case to case.

The manipulative projection of C into E is originally performed by the creative artist in producing the work of art. It is then performed by the interpreter (in the case of the performing arts) in reproducing the work according to plans (scripts, scores, etc.) laid down by the creative artist. Finally the same cycle is performed by the appreciator who thus manipulates his environment in relation to himself that he is exposed to the finished work. Going to a gallery or concert hall is much the same kind of aesthetic activity as buying the canvas or the musical instrument. It is preparatory to obtaining the P's which could conform to one's aesthetic C's. Viewing pictures or listening to musical performances; putting paint on canvas or producing tones on instruments, are all purposive manipulative activities whereby one's invariant aesthetic vision or design is constructively projected into the relevant environment. The sum of these projections constitutes the environment as a world fraught with aesthetic meaning; and this is the 'effective environment' of the arts.

Speaking of 'invariance' in regard to such ephemeral things as aesthetic sensibility or vision may seem objectionable. Yet in fact it is no more so than speaking of invariance with respect to the Lorentz transformation-formulas in physics. No physicist would seriously maintain that these LT's (as they are referred to) are invariant in the sense that they shall always figure in physical theories. They merely hold that, as long as they are used, they are invariant in regard to the phenomena to which they apply, i.e. which may be mathematically shown to be their transformations. Similarly in the case of aesthetic C's. The fact that on listening to a Chopin Nocturne I am conscious of a lucid and satisfying feeling does not mean that henceforth I must always enjoy Chopin Nocturnes. It only means that I now possess the aesthetic C's which 'de-code' the sounds of the Nocturne. The C's are the codes which make a given work of art (or natural scene) aesthetically significant. They do so in virtue of the fact that they represent ways or forms of lucid feeling, which the actual perceptions fill with content. We are 'feeling as' thus significant the particular work of art we behold. The P's afforded by the work (colors, sounds, etc.) appear as particular transformations of our ways of feeling; the latter represent the invariance which underlies the transformations. It is because of this invariance that I can enjoy two different Nocturnes, or the same Nocturne performed by different artists, or other works by Chopin, or even romantic music by a composer other than Chopin. But beyond a given limit the sounds I hear are no longer felt as transformations of the aesthetic invariance in question, and just because I have an appreciation of Chopin no longer guarantees that I enjoy Bartok. A closely related, but perhaps somewhat different C

is required for that purpose. And this brings us to the adaptive phase of the aesthetic feedback cycle.

(28)

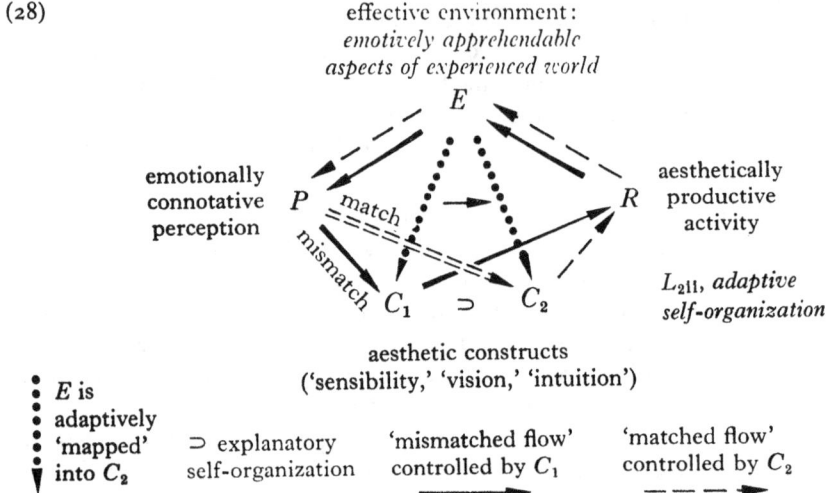

In the above diagram (which is a familiar one by now) C_1 represents the 'problem': an aesthetic construct which proves to be unsatisfactory in view of our actual exposure to an instance of art or natural scenery ('mismatch signal'). By means of free-running activities, various C's can be explored as 'hypotheses.' Thus an aesthetic learning-process takes place which, if successful, evolves our taste and sensibility, and permits us to enjoy scenes and styles which were hitherto unfamiliar and aesthetically barren ('match signal' replaces 'mismatch signal'). We learn to 'map' the aesthetically significant qualities of yet another state or aspect of the environment. Hence stylistic change can be accounted for. The creative artist evolves C's which are beyond those of his time and place. His creation is puzzling at first, and perhaps displeasing. If it is a true artistic creation, however, in the sense that it is the embodiment of a genuine discovery of feeling, it is entirely possible that others will also develop the C's which inspired its creation. The public can 'learn' to appreciate it. It thereby acquires the codes which unlock the aesthetic significance of the style and manner of work of the creative artist.[1] A new aesthetic era is ushered in.

[1] This formulation of aesthetic learning should not mislead the reader to think of it as a process of concept-formation. The C's in question are types and sequences of meaningful and lucid feelings, and the discovery, that a given set of perceptions 'expresses' such feeling is non-conceptual, similarly to 'insight-learning' in children and animals.

This seldom means that old C's are dropped₁out and that, as a consequence we fail to appreciate traditional art and patterns of significance. Rather, the new aesthetic C's are added to the old and we are enriched by a new faculty for appreciating the beauty and emotive meaning of our experience.

By developing new aesthetic constructs, and then projecting them into our environment to bring our perceptions to accord with them, we are slowly but surely making our surroundings aesthetically more satisfying. If alone aesthetic constructs would guide our actions, our environment would be one of beauty and harmony. This was typical of ages, such as the Hellenic, when aesthetic C's were dominant. In the present age, however, much of our activities are guided by scientific constructs. Thereby we create surroundings in which almost all things that we encounter are manipulable, predictable and controllable—if not in actual fact, then in principle. The puzzling observational and experimental situation is the exception rather than the rule. (This holds true even if we admit that such situations may be important in providing the springboard for processes of learning.) But our rationally and empirically known environmental objects do not necessarily satisfy our craving for an aesthetic order in the realm of our emotive apprehension of reality—our 'life of feeling.' Thus much of the contemporary landscape—the technologized cities and machine-subdued lands—are aesthetically deficient, notwithstanding the steady growth of our storehouses of aesthetic constructs and even of their external embodiments. The meaning of 'technological age' is that the external embodiments of rational constructs predominate over the embodiments of aesthetic ideals.

(c) Meta-Sensory Feedback: L_{2111} (Religious Activity)

Cultural man requires intelligibility in his stream of experience to an extent which transcends the intrinsic potentials of sensory *Gestalten* in two principal respects. The first of these, the requirements for deductively formulated interrelations between sense-perceived events, is answered by science. The second, the need for harmony and meaning in his emotional life, is the province of art. What, then, are we to make of religion?

There are many philosophies of religion, past and present. I shall discuss but one of them: the naturalistic theory espoused among others by Whitehead and William James, which is directly relevant to my empirical-rational interpretation of human experience. Accordingly, we note that in the history of human culture numerous occasions have presented themselves wherein feelings arose which proved to be incapable of elucidation either by the art or by the science of the period. Such feelings appear to demand an explanation in terms of realities lying *beyond* the perceived world of everyday experience. For example, there are the recurrent historical reports of a feeling of divine or supernatural presence. Whether or not we agree to the validity of such feelings, as signifying a real, although 'non-natural' presence, has little to do with our commitment to recognize the reality of the feeling itself. Introspectively reported sensations are unfalsifiable, and if a significant number of people throughout the ages reported such feelings, the reality of the feelings cannot be doubted or ignored. They are recurrent items in human experience. We accept the historical evidence for the occurrence of such feelings and attempt to elucidate the pattern of cognition and behavior resulting in reference to it through our basic information-flow scheme. Thus I note that the passage from P (feeling of transcendental significance) to C (invariant supernatural event of entity) is analogous to the $P \rightarrow C$ passages in other spheres of meta-sensory activity, including art and science. Although at first blush this claim may seem unacceptable to scientists, it is in fact explicitly confirmed by at least one eminent physicist. Margenau states, 'From the point of view of epistemology the theologian who seeks the "rule" for passing from an immediate experience of religious awe to a divine presence is doing precisely the same as the neurologist who correlates this feeling with a certain condition of the nervous system; and both are attempting what the physicist does when he associates a wavelength with a color sensation.'[1] I might add to this that all three are doing precisely what the artist does when he assimilates the sounds of the Ninth Symphony's final theme to the feeling of supreme joy and triumph. In all these instances a passage takes place from perceived sensation to meta-sensory construction, in accordance with 'rules' resulting from the person's patterns of enculturation. The specific characteristic of the empirical datum of religion is that it is not a *seeing* (as in science) but a *feeling*, and that it is not a feeling *as* (as in art) but a feeling *that* . . . In this view, the roots of religion lie in a feeling which refers beyond itself and demands comprehension in terms of constructs with which it is epistemically correlated.

This assessment of the nature of religion accords with the views of James as well as Whitehead. Take, for example, Whitehead's assertion that religion is 'an ultimate craving to infuse into the insistent particularity of emotion that non-temporal generality which primarily belongs to conceptual thought alone.'[2] Here a 'feeling *that*' functions as an insistently particular emotion, and a transcendent construct as the non-temporal generality belonging primarily to conceptual thought. Hence the systems of ideas in theologies become conceptual explanations—or justifications—

[1] Margenau, *The Nature of Physical Reality*, op. cit., p. 62.
[2] Whitehead, *Process and Reality*, op. cit., p. 23.

of emotional experience. Religion, then, has its roots in feelings and its superstructure in general ideas. James reviewed numerous reports of such feelings and concluded that 'the whole array of our instances leads to a conclusion something like this: It is as if there were in the human consciousness a *sense of reality, a feeling of objective presence, a perception* of what we may call "*something there*," more deep and more general than any of the special and particular "senses" by which current psychology supposes existent realities to be originally revealed.'[1] This phenomenon James subsequently calls 'sense of presence.' He explicitly names it a religious *feeling*. He would agree, I believe, with the view that it is essentially a 'feeling *that*.' The transcendental nature of the feeling validates the 'rule of correspondence' in a given theology, by means of which we pass from the feeling itself (the 'sense of presence') to the religious concept (divine being or supernatural event). Once in the realm of concepts, the rational mind takes over and derives further concepts from those implied by the feeling and provides systematic connection between the concepts. Thus there are systematic sets of 'religious constructs' which make up particular theologies. Some of these constructs are 'operationally defined' (by means of rules of correspondence with religious feelings) and others are 'constitutively defined' (through rules of logical inference to other religious constructs, some of which have been operationally defined). Hence the theoretical edifice of theology is not radically different from that of science, *beyond the nature of the original inference*. That inference, however, is very different. It is based on feeling in theology, and on observation in science. It is summed up in the contrast between '*feeling* that' and '*seeing* that.' Were it not for observation, science could hardly be said to be capable of existing. Similarly, had religious feelings not existed, theology and religious philosophy could not have developed. James tells us that 'feeling is the deeper source of religion, and ... philosophic and theological formulas are secondary products, like translations of a text into another tongue ... I mean that in a world in which no religious feeling had ever existed, I doubt whether any philosophic theology could ever have been framed.' Theological speculations, James holds, must 'be classed as over-beliefs, buildings-out performed by the intellect into directions of which feeling originally supplied the hint.'[2] This discussion shows that religion is based on an element discovered in the stream of human experience and that this element is correlated with a concept or idea, which represents our assessment of its transcendental significance. The element in experience belongs to P and it is by nature a feeling. The concept or idea belongs to C, and it

---

[1] William James, *The Varieties of Religious Experience*, London, 1904, p. 58.
[2] James, *op. cit.*, p. 431.

is what I call a 'religious construct.' P and C are correlated by means of rules of correspondence evolved within a religious sect or culture group, so that whenever P obtains a typical member of the group passes to the correlated religious C and from thence to the rest of the adopted theology (or as much of it as he is familiar with and accepts). This presupposes the naturalistic interpretation of religion, inasmuch as other interpretations may not locate the experiential basis of theologies in transcedentally significative feelings. But it is worthy of passing comment that, although other philosophies of religion may disagree with this particular interpretation, they may nevertheless prove to be compatible with the present information-flow design of religious cognition and activity. That design conserves the invariant relationship of the key terms of the system and acquires, in this particular interpretation, the following values:

(29)

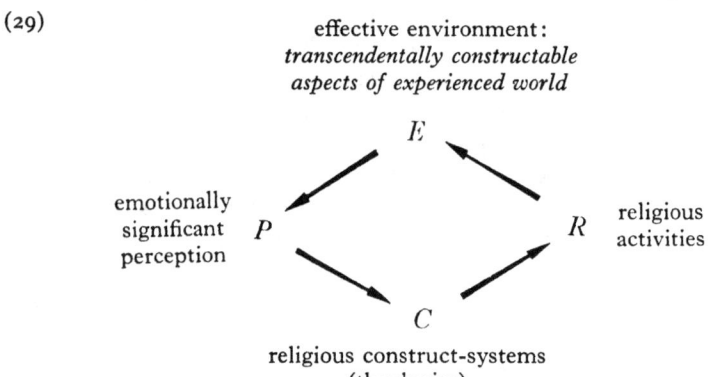

L_{2III}, general information-flow

The empirical basis of religion lies, according to the above scheme, in an emotively significant perception (a 'feeling *that*') connected, by means of a rule of correspondence postulated by a system of transcendental religious constructs, to that system itself. The response made to the experience is thus not merely a response to the religious constructs with which it is immediately connected through the 'rule,' but to the system of constructs in which the given C is a component (this is much the same in the case of other systems of constructs). For example, the 'sense of presence,' whether occurring in a religious ceremony or more randomly in the context of everyday life, calls forth a response not merely to a given construct, like the presence of a supernatural being, but to the entire system of religion which identifies the being and places it within the context of its system. Thus at Lourdes, Bernadette responded to the Holy Virgin of Christian theology, and not to an unknown supernatural woman; and at communion the devout Catholic responds to the flesh and blood of Christ and not to an unconnected feeling of transcendental significance.

Response occurs to religious feeling but, it may be objected, it is non-deliberate and undirected. This one may grant on the plane of *random* religious experiences. But are not many, if not most of our religious experiences highly organized? Religion is institutionalized in all civilized societies and religious experiences tend to occur on the designated times and places, namely *in* the places of worship and *on* the days of worship. When experiences of a religious kind, such as having a 'sense of presence' even in a mild form (e.g. as a sense of awe or transcendent beauty) occur outside these occasions, our reponses to them tend to be non-deliberate and undirected. We may stand dumbfounded, or exclaim in delight. But when our religious experiences are had *in* the context of religious ceremonial, our responses are highly deliberate and clearly directed; they maintain, or modify, the cult or ceremonial. In fact, the ceremonial itself is a collective response to the religious experiences generated by it. If this implies a circularity it is well: for here is where we encounter feedback in religious activity. I can best analyze it in terms of the circuits of manipulative self-stabilization and adaptive self-organization outlined in the foregoing sections.

(30)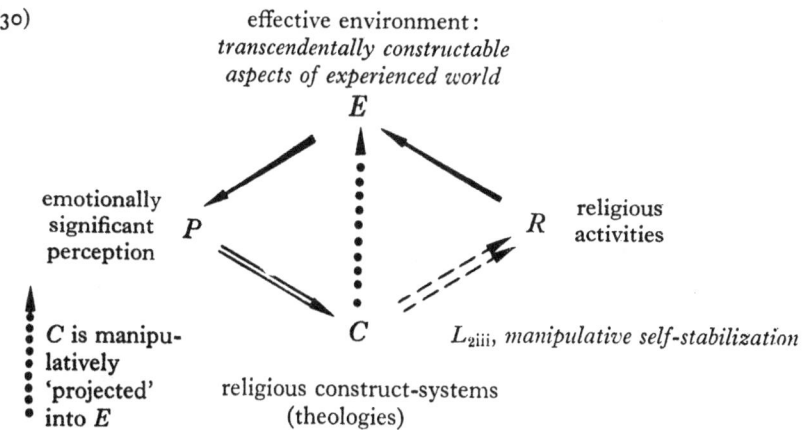

In the representation of the manipulative phase, R stands for purposively directed response to religious experience. The response produces ex periences relevant to those undergone; thus religious activity obtains in response to religious experience and is designed to bring about such experience. It accomplishes this by the building of shrines, altars, and buildings as places of worship and location of ceremony; by devising and performing the ceremony and by using such ritual accessories which strengthen the religious experience. The tolling of bells, burning of incense, the robes, the chants, and the many other correlates of a cult, create a total experiential pattern which is dedicated to one thing: the production of states of the environment which, when perceived, satisfy the constructs of the theological system. Thus, consistently with other facets of human experience, religious activity can be said to 'project' its codes into the relevant environment. It (in other words) acts on the environment in function of producing experiences analyzable as transformations of invariant religious constructs. The resulting religious experience consists in a feeling, triggered by carefully coordinated sights, sounds, smells and movements, which functions as the particular transformation of an invariant religious construct. The latter may be a key concept denoting a supernatural being, or merely a subsidiary one, such as the notion of purification of sins by the confessional. When individual experience conforms to any such invariant theological concept, it has established the invariance of the given religion in the individual's experience. The thus reinforced C's, systematically correlated with others in the theological system, serve as the ground for new responses, having further impact on the environment and tending to produce further invariances of the theology in experience. Thus, by means of R, religious experience is self-stabilizing, precisely as are the other circuits of human activity.

The adaptive self-organization of religious activity (figure 31):

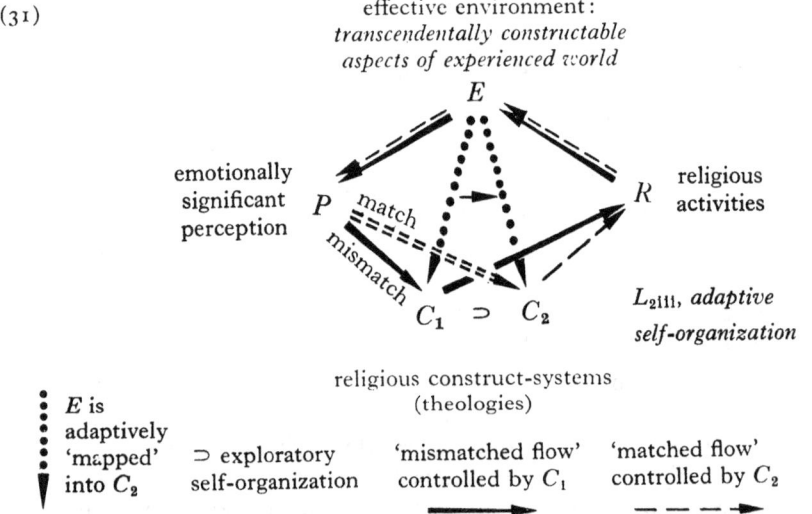

provides for 'learning' and flexibility under changing patterns of religious experience. It permits the development of C's whereby religious experiences which do not fit the established constructs can be accounted for. If a 'feeling *that*' becomes prevalent in a given group which has no religious constructs to interpret it ('problem'), pressure is exerted on the existing constructs to accomodate the new experience. The existing constructs are either extended or replaced ('hypothesis'). Whether the one or the other occurs determines whether an existing religion is further evolved, or a new religion (or a new form of the old religion) takes its place. The history of religion provides ample examples of both these processes. Whether by revolution, reformation, or evolution, theological systems evolve a set of C's, controlling matched information-flows, in terms of which coordinated responses may be produced, leading to a confirmation of the C's in experience. Religious systems must be adaptive if they are to perpetuate themselves: they must learn to map the changing types of religious feelings of the culture in their theologies. (The lack of such adaptability may, incidentally, be the key problem of the present-day Church, and the reason why young people turn to Oriental construct-systems for elucidation.)

Because of the circularity inherent in the above process, religion was often accused of setting out to prove its premises in its conclusions. However, while this is true, we may say in defense of religion that science, art, and even ordinary sensory activity, does essentially the same. The difference lies merely in the nature of the experience that is proven. For religion it is a feeling which carries, in its very nature, the germs of faith in the reality of that of which the feeling is a 'feeling that.' Fundamentalism is based on the recognition of this fact. It bases its argument on an unquestioning faith, which is an unconditional recognition of the reality of the 'that' involved in religious experience. The logical arguments whereby God's existence and the validity of all constructs in a theological system are 'proven' presuppose the acceptance of religious experience, i.e. unquestioning faith, the same way as the theoretical constructions of science presuppose the acceptance of the rationalistic significance of observational and experimental evidence. Fundamentalist theology, therefore, sets out to prove its axiomatically accepted premises and does this, over and above purely logical proofs, by the 'experimental' method of reproducing the premises under controlled conditions: reproducing a religious feeling serving as the basis of faith, under conditions of prescribed ceremonial. But science does much the same in regard to *its* premises, namely the observational and experimental protocol data: it reproduces them under controlled conditions, thereby validating the unperceived, and often unperceivable, system of constructs on the basis of which the data were predicted.

Operational confirmation is inherently circular. It confirms, by manipulating the environment, the C's on the basis of which there is manipulation. In homeostasis we confirm our physiological codes by projecting them into the internal environment: thus there is a stable organic structure. In everyday activity we confirm our sense-codes by projecting them into the extradermal environment: thus we find ourselves in a world of knowable sense-objects. In science we confirm our rational–empirical scientific constructs by projecting them, through scientific observation and experimentation, into the natural universe: it is thus that we discover the natural principles, laws and entities of this world. The activities associated with art confirm our aesthetic-constructs in our environment by the purposive creation of aesthetic objects and works of art. And, last but not least, in religious activity our religious feelings find confirmation through rites and ceremonials which lend our surroundings transcendental significance. There is circularity, but it is one which is inherent in all aspects of cognitive experience as a variously coded, multilevel feedback process operating on the basis of the homeostatic feedback-circuit to which all living things owe their existence, but transcending it in the successively superimposed circuits, coded so as to complete a gap or unsatisfactory vagueness inherent in the one below. Thereby the higher circuits organize the lower ones, and our consciousness of our mental activity ascends to, and primarily infuses, the higher loops. It is in terms of science, art and religion that we tend to view ourselves and our world, for our total pattern of activity is coded on the highest, and therefore controlling, level. Thus, although the various levels of cognition and activity are genetically continuous, they develop autonomy on their respective levels and become irreducible to the ones below. It is nonsense to speak of a scientific construct as a code which is instrumental to the homeostasis of the scientist's organism, but it makes sense to hold that the information-flow pattern of the scientist, as he postulates his hypotheses and proceeds to test and confirm them, is isomorphic to the flow pattern of his physiological regulatory processes, but occurs on a higher plane, capable of deriving more information from his environment than the homeostatic circuit. Thus there is continuity from below and irreducibility from above. The multiple levels of human experience evolved in a continuous sweep, but interrelate, when evolved, in virtue of the hierarchically organized structural isomorphism of their patterns of information-flow. In the hierarchy the higher levels are more 'analytic' of the system's environmental states: they represent more accurate as well as more far-reaching correlations between such states and the system's codes. Invariances are discovered with respect to more, and more diverse, types of perceptions; more information is derived from the environment. The cultural person has rational, aesthetic as well as religious codes, and finds his experience intelligible in regard to factors which lapse into undifferentiated or merely chaotic 'noise' for the non-cultured organism. Thus culture signifies a more detailed knowledge of the environment in relation to the person and as such has distinct survival value for the species. Yet the cultural circuits gain autonomy, and cultural man engages in science, art, religion and related activities not merely to live, but also to understand himself and his world. Intelligence is generated by a survival need but becomes self-perpetuating and self-improving in the process.

The account of cognitive experience given in this chapter involves the lower rungs (L_0, L_1, L_2) of a potentially infinite hierarchy. These levels deal with some aspect of empirical actuality, i.e. their codes are mappings of states of a presumably objective reality 'outside' the mind. However, these are not the only kinds of cognitions there are and thus, before concluding this chapter, I should say some words about extending the hierarchy to account for *reflective* cognition. (A detailed study of this area requires a book in itself, however, and must await another occasion.)

Beyond L_2 in the hierarchy of cognitive experience, the codes of the circuits are representations or mappings of other codes, rather than of states of the environment. Specifically, for a circuit of level L_n, the 'effective environment' (E) is the set of codes (*Gestalten*, constructs) of level L_{n-1}, and cognition involves the correlation of its own codes (C) with states of that set, both by learning to map its invariances (i.e. adaptively) and by causing such configurations to occur which correspond to one's ideas of the set (manipulatively). The codes confirmed in L_n may in turn become the 'effective environment' of a cognitive circuit on level L_{n+1}, the codes of which are mappings of the L_n codes; and so on. Since each level circuit can be reflected upon, we get an infinite regress. In such a series only level L_3 is of particular interest: it contains the information-flows of much of philosophy (this book, with the exception of the present paragraph [which is L_4] is an L_3 construct-system), most of psychology, and of the 'theories ("philosophies") *of*' any cognate discipline, including mathematics (in the intuitionist view). Thereafter the levels progressively reduce to increasingly difficult and unproductive feats of introspection. (Thinking of thinking of thinking of . . .x.)

CHAPTER 4

Multilevel Interpersonal Communication

At first glance the foregoing analyses may have given the impression that the diverse levels of human experience, although coexisting for most cultural persons, are somehow discrete, so that one operates at a given time to the exclusion of the others. This impression is justified only in regard to the 'pure' cognitive activities wherewith I exemplified the arguments. The scientist in his laboratory, the artist in his studio, the priest in his church, are immersed in one predominant type of feedback-controlled pattern of cognition and response. But outside of these occasions, most men integrate the various cognitive modes in heterogeneous thought and action processes.

Consider the examples given in Chapter 2. The simple case of 'light falls on my eyelids and I open my eyes' is a 'pure' experiential mode: it is one which involves the homeostatic circuit where the state of a part of the internal environment is sensed (the sensation of greater light intensity on the optical sensors gives rise to neural stimuli) and the corresponding physiological responses (issuing in my opening my eyes) are correlated with the event. The sunflower does essentially the same when it turns toward the light. But when we set forth the example and say '. . . and see a sunlit tree' we leave the sunflower behind. We then penetrate into the realm of the sensory cognition of external (extra-dermal) events. The various patterns of light are assimilated to an invariant and familiar *Gestalt*, the tree, notwithstanding that I may never have seen this particular tree in this particular light and from this particular angle before. The sunflower cannot do this, but an animal can. (Whether or not his *Gestalt* 'tree' is the same as mine is another question.) Now, if I become aware of a sensation of hunger and get up and walk toward home, I am mixing two different experiential modes, operating on distinct circuits of self-stabilization and organization. The sensory *Gestalt* 'tree' becomes interrelated with other *Gestalten* in the perceptually cognized common-sense environment, and one of these *Gestalten* is the food which my getting up and walking away is designed to reach. The other mode is the sensation of hunger, interrelated with the expected sensation of satisfaction upon eating. The two modes, the perceptual–cognitive and the homeostatic, interpenetrate and guide my actions jointly. Animals who habitually search out their food perform precisely such an operation, in the hybrid mode of homeostatic *and* perceptual–behavioral circuits.

Now further suppose that my action is motivated by my remembering that at 2 p.m. I have an appointment and should be finished with lunch by then. The notion 'appointment at 2 p.m.' is not an observable: I can perceive neither '2 p.m.' nor 'appointment.' But it is the kind of rational construction which interrelates many things which I can and do perceive, such as the presence of the man I am to see and the hands on the face of my watch. Thus '2 p.m. appointment' is a variety of scientific construct, although in the technical sense it does not belong to any given science but has been adopted as part of the ordinary common-sense sequence of events. Feelings of aesthetic enjoyment and of religious significance may likewise be intertwined in even such a simple experience as perceiving a sunlit tree. In all such cases the highest of animals has been outstripped in intellectual and cultural acuity: animals do not entertain rational, aesthetic or religious constructs. The cultural level is typically human, and for cultural persons it is part and parcel of their everyday experience.

In the above examples only one person, the subject, was involved. But in another example, likewise mentioned in Chapter 2, I proposed 'perceiving a patrolman in the rearview mirror and slowing down to avoid getting a speeding ticket.' This example can be laid out as a potential *communication* between two individual persons: the patrolman and the subject. The behavioral response 'I slow down to avoid getting a ticket' makes reference to a cognitive activity circuit integrating two modes: the perceptual, dictating the bodily actions in reference to such perceptions as the road, the position of the car relative to it and to other traffic, etc., and the rational-scientific, incorporating the 'seeing *that*' my speedometer shows a speed higher than that posted on roadside signs. The latter component makes reference to an unobservable construct: velocity. To be sure, moving bodies are observables, but bodies moving at the speed of 60 miles per hour are not. '60 m.p.h.' is a rational construct, permitting the axiomatic manipulation of objects perceived in the guise of sensory *Gestalten*. In this, it is similar to 'appointment at 2 p.m.' But in the present example my behavioral response is dictated by the presence of another person, namely, the approaching patrolman. Thus it interrelates with his cognitive activity circuits. He too, I must presume, operates at this moment primarily on two levels of cognition: the perceptual, distinguishing sensory objects, which include my car, and the scientific, relating his observations to rational constructs, such as speed limits. A communication, implicit in our respective acts of cognition and response, thus involves two basic experiential modes, although it by no means excludes others as additional components.

If he should stop me, the ensuing discussion would involve sensory *Gestalten*, such as cars, road, and so on, with heavy reference to rational constructs, such as public safety, speed limits, clocked velocities, etc. Note now that much of the latter relies not on direct perceptions but on *symbols*. Not only is the language we are talking a symbol for our meanings, but our meanings themselves are often symbols, rather than the 'real' things. (The posted speed limit is a symbol for the real speed with which one may travel, the license for driving ability, etc.) While it is possible to say, for example, that I merely compared two perceptual *Gestalten* in slowing down, the sign outside posting the speed limit and the pointer on my speedometer, and what I did was to establish a relation of equivalence between them, this description leaves out the entire meaning of the act, namely the obeying of traffic rules. Such rules, as for example '60 m.p.h. speed limit' are symbolized by the roadside sign's legend 'speed limit 60' and my obedience to it is symbolized, in reference to the actual velocity of my vehicle, by the speedometer.

Even such a simple occurrence as checking one's speed against a posted limit involves symbolized meanings. A communication between two persons, in this case between the patrolman and the subject, thus proceeds on multiple levels one or both of which includes symbols. 'Seeing' in 'seeing *as*' and especially in 'seeing *that*' may refer not to the event which is seen 'as' and 'that,' but to the *symbol* of the event. Looking at one's watch and seeing that he is late, looking at the speedometer and seeing that he is exceeding the limit, are not seeing the time and the velocity of one's vehicle, but the symbols for time and the symbols for speed. The integration of symbols with the 'real things,' together with the integration of different levels of cognition and response, must all be taken into account when dealing with communication between two or more persons.

Let us attempt now an adequate theoretical formulation of these factors. In order to have intercommunication between two persons, one must have communication capability in each of the persons involved. Thus *inter*-personal communication presupposes *intra*personal communication. Intra-personal communication may be conceived as the derivation of information by an individual from his environment. Our self-stabilizing self-organizing circuits do precisely that. They satisfy the standard notions of communication, as evidenced also by the fact that they can be directly reinterpreted as communication-systems. Take for example Thayer's definition of 'communication.' Thayer does not conceive of communication as a uniquely human phenomenon but as one of the two basic life processes (the other one being the acquisition and processing of energy). 'Just as the crucial component of physical metabolism is the conversion of raw environmental processes into energy forms consumable or processable by a particular living system, the crucial component of the communication process is the conversion of raw event-*data* into forms of *information* consumable or processable by that living system.'[1] He then defines communication as 'all those processes associated with the acquisition and conversion of raw event-data into consumable or processable information, culminating in an instance of taking-something-into-account.'[2] In Thayer's system 'raw event-data' are equivalent to my 'input' and their processing as information pertinent to the system equals my 'coding.' In fact, both the manipulative and adaptive functions of my system are outlined by Thayer as components of communication, the former as a process which is *morphostatic*, and the latter one which is *morphogentic* in character.[3] Consequently the multilevel feedback system proposed on these pages can be seen to constitute a communication system of the *intrapersonal* variety. If I am to propose a model of *inter*personal communication, then, I must bring two or more such intrapersonally communicating circuits into mutual relation. I shall do this by outlining an optimally simple model of interpersonal communication, in which two communicating systems interact. Each communicating system is a complete multilevel feedback system with codes and matching circuits ranging from basic homeostasis, through perceptual cognition, to the metalevels of cultural cognitive activites. For the sake of simplicity and clarity I shall speak of one such system as the 'agent' (sender) and of the second as the 'Other' (receiver). The model does not preclude that more than two communicating systems should be involved but represents a conceptualization of the sender-receiver optimally simple instance of *interpersonal* communication.[4]

---

[1] Lee Thayer, 'Communication—*Sine Qua Non* of the Behavioral Sciences' in *Vistas in Science*, University of New Mexico Press, 1968, p. 52.

[2] *Ibid*, p. 58.

[3] *Ibid*, p. 60.

[4] Thayer speaks of a series of levels of analysis in which the interpersonal is but one level. His levels include:

'(a) the intrapersonal (the point of focus being one individual, and the dynamics of communication as such);

(b) the interpersonal (the point of focus being a two or more person interactive system and its properties—the process of intercommunication and its concomitants);

The basic problem to consider is, how communication can take place between the systems. Each of the circuits must in some respects be 'open' to the other. On surveying them we can readily conclude that only one element in each circuit *can* be open to another circuit, and that is E, the environment. The other elements—input, codes, output—appear to be private for each circuit (person).

But even the assumption that an 'Other' can be an element in 'my' environment needs to be qualified. On a more careful analysis it becomes evident that the Other can enter into the agent's (or 'my') *extra-dermal* environment only, including the emotionally connoted, signified, and the empirical–rationalistically inferred mappings of it. The Other cannot enter into my bodily environment, for such entry conflicts with the cogent use of 'my.' As long as I appropriate for myself one part of my environment and say that 'it is I,' there can be no relations of *that* environment with 'others.' But this 'windowlessness' is due to a restriction imposed on one part of E, and not to a categorical schism between that environment and the continuum beyond it. The spectrum of my 'effective environment' extends in an unbroken continuum from my body to the furthest reaches of the universe, but I cannot share my *milieu intérieur* segment of it with others. This is what is meant when we say that '*I* feel *my* headache but you cannot.' I obtain a P from that part of my environment called 'my head' whereas you cannot get such a perception (discounting ESP and empathy).

Turning to the positive or *open* side of E, we can note that each of its remaining mappings is readily shared. My sense-perceived extra-dermal environment can be that of the Other and, provided the Other likewise constructs his perceptions by means of scientific, aesthetic and religious constructs, the natural universe in which I find myself through my scientific activity, as well as the worlds of art and religion, disclosed to me in virtue of my aesthetic and religious cognitions, are also those which obtain for the Other. The worlds of common-sense, science, art and religion are public worlds capable of being analogously mapped by different individuals; the world of the body alone is private. (The latter being due, I repeat, to the

---

(c) the multi-person human enterprise level (the point of focus being the internal structure and functioning of multi-person human enterprises);

(d) the enterprise↔environment level (the point of focus being upon the interface between human organizations and their environments); and

(e) the technological level of analysis (the focus being upon the efficacy of those technologies—both hardware and software—which have evolved in the service of man's communication and intercommunication endeavors).'

Ibid., p. 56.

fact that no perceptions can be had of the internal environment by any 'other' person.)

The environment is not a direct component in our conscious apprehension of experience: it is communicated to us through perceptions and the perceptions are heavily laden with constructions. Seeing, as I emphasized, is not just a simple matter, but always seeing *as* or seeing *that*. And it is thus with *feeling* as well. Plain seeing, and feeling, would be an enigma: it would be a mere cognizance of our sensory data (including their emotional coloring). But these data are unique and perishing; as Plato, Hume and Kant pointed out (and their observation is independent of the theories they advanced when confronted with it), there is no systematic knowledge—and in fact no knowledge in a meaningful sense—of sensory impressions by themselves. Something more is required—a phase of synthesis or construction—before the exteroceptive, emotionally charged signals become fraught with intelligibility. And this something I identified as our *Gestalt*-systems, scientific, aesthetic and religious constructs and construct systems. By means of them the events of the external world can be mapped into our nervous system.

Now, to interrelate the experience of the agent and the Other, they need a common E. But to effect some degree of communication of *knowledge* between them, they also need common types of sense organs, assuring analogous P's, and common types of mentality, guaranteeing that the P's will be analogously referred. Lastly, they need common behavior patterns, so that the analogous C's could issue in similar responses, feeding back to E. In this analysis I shall assume that common predominant types of mappings (perceptive apparatus, mentality and behavior patterns) evolve in common cultural and societal environments. That is, I place the brunt of the argument on a common E and hold that the other factors tend to group themselves in basically analogous ways around it. This is to draw on sociological and anthropological evidence which, abstracting from specific detail, shows that predominant types of behavior and common modes of cognition emerge in groups sharing the same environment. On this basis I assume that our sender and receiver (the agent and the Other), belonging to the same species and to the same historical–social group, analogously map their environment (have similar types of 'effective environment').

But is the assumption of a *common environment* fully tenable? Can the E, even when stripped of its bodily component, be entirely shared between the agent and the Other (or others)? If we turn to physics for an answer, we get an unhesitating 'no.' Relativity theory asserts that each observer in the four-dimensional space–time continuum has a unique position. He splits the continuum into three dimensions of space and one of time according to his unique position and gets a unique environment in consequence. Each observer, being a single point-event in this capacity, follows his own world-line. Individual world-lines may intersect, but do not merge. Whitehead, inspired by the relativity principle, tells us that 'each actual occasion defines it own actual world from which it originates. No two occasions can have identical actual worlds.'[1]

If Einstein and Whitehead are right, the assumption, that the environment is fully shared between the agent and the Other, is false. The E which appears for the one is not the E which appears for the other. Since perceptions derive from the respective E's, the P's of different observers will also be specifically differentiated. When you and I behold the same picture, you see it from a standpoint different from mine. Moreover, even if we exchanged places, our total perceptions would differ: the universe did not still its course in the intervening time—and in addition, our own bodily sets would also be different. Generalizing from physics, one can maintain that no two total perceptual fields are exactly alike, due to the shift, however slight, of the relation between world and percipient.

The differences may be large, or they may be negligible. They tend to be the latter when the agent and the Other are in fact perceiving the same things as well as each other. Corrections can be made for the differing standpoints and bodily sets and the term E can be *de facto* shared. But it will not be *actually* shared: there will still be some difference between the E's which figure in the two circuits of experience. This argument leads me to acknowledge an *analogy* between the E's, and not an *identity*. The analogy obtains when we inspect the same environment from the respective (and differing) viewpoints of sender and receiver.

The analogy can be resolved into identity only if we adopt the external analyst's position and consider that the communicators may be sharing the same natural region (extended space-time area). Unless we allow for extended loci in the natural universe, we cannot meaningfully speak of a shared 'here-and-now,' since all loci become reduced to space-time point events. Bowing to the necessity of using such an idealization for practical purposes, and not wishing to surrender exactitude in the face of it, I shall denote the physical space–time point locus of sender and receiver with '*environment*' (with a lower case 'e') and symbolize the extended space–time region which both communicators may share with '*Environment*' (with a capital 'E'). We thus get analogous environments for sender and receiver making up part of an identical Environment. This method of schematization enables me to maintain that the self-stabilizing and self-organizing

[1] A. N. Whitehead, *Process and Reality*, op. cit. Cf. especially *Categories of Explanation* (v) and (vi).

activities of agent and Other result in analogous states of their respective environments, and in an identical state of their common Environment. Each person orders the states of his environment in accordance with his codes and constructs, projecting these into the Environment as external embodiments.

The environment of one interrelates, through the Environment, with the environment of the other. The circuits acquire 'windows' as the ordering activities of different individuals effect commonly ordered states in one another's environments. Thus the character of the Environment is a social product, individually elaborated. In it the typical patterns of cultural civilization prevail, emergent from the mutually conditioned circuits of individual activity.

Now, in the progressive complexification of the culturally ordered Environment, modes of manipulation and communication are evolved which *represent*, rather than *exhibit* the intended element of order. I am referring to symbols.[1] In this context symbol must be sharply differentiated from sign. A sign is an event A whose occurrence is accompanied by an event B. Contrarily, a symbol need not be accompanied by the event it symbolizes—it denotes that event and takes its place in experience. Thus, whereas signs can be established by an invariant association between two events, where one functions as the sign of the other (as in conditioned reflexes), symbols require a degree of abstraction. The perceived symbol denotes the unperceived event by means of a preestablished convention. Due to the relative freedom of establishing such conventions, symbolization can vastly facilitate communication.

Consider the Environmental event *forest*. Although the wider Environment of most agents in our societies include forests, forests do not always enter in the environments (i.e. into the immediate experience) of all agents. Sometimes we experience a forest and often we do not. But it is convenient to represent the *Gestalt* 'forest' as well as the scientific construct 'forest' (and perhaps also the aesthetic and religious constructs 'forest') whenever desired. This can be done by entertaining the corresponding codes in one's mind. But the codes thus entertained are private. Their communication and interpersonal manipulation presuppose their 'embodiment' in the Environment. Hereby they become data in the experience of the Other (and of all others who share that Environment) and become further referred to meanings analogous to that of the agent. If you entertain the code 'forest' and wish me to share it, you can take me to a forest and point to it. But this may be inconvenient. It is simpler to

[1] Here 'symbol' stands for the embodied Environmental object and not its cognitive meaning: the latter is a C (construct).

utter the word 'forest' or to write it down for me. I shall then behold six oddly contorted black lines on a white sheet, or hear a short bark-like sound, but, remarkably enough, will refer these perceptions to trees. This is the power and the function of embodied symbols. By convention, they function as vouchers in place of the experiences which they symbolize.

In my exposition to this point I have taken account of the difficulties of communication between two cultural persons, i.e. multiply coded self-stabilizing and self-organizing systems. The difficulties arise due to the fact that not one of the component terms is entirely shared, and even that component which is at least analogous for any two persons in a given setting is partially symbolized, and thus cluttered with conventional meanings. The convenience of communication increases in direct proportion to the decrease of its accuracy.

These ideas may be represented in the information-flow chart of *intra*personal communications, using identically coded symbols and non-symbolized environmental events:

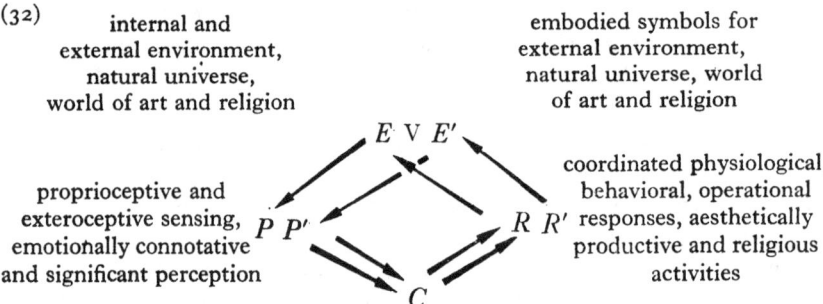

(32)

| internal and external environment, natural universe, world of art and religion | | embodied symbols for external environment, natural universe, world of art and religion |

proprioceptive and exteroceptive sensing, emotionally connotative and significant perception

coordinated physiological, behavioral, operational responses, aesthetically productive and religious activities

physiological codes, *Gestalten*, scientific, aesthetic and religious constructs

Intrapersonal Communication: *general information-flow*

In order to obtain the general information-flow chart of *inter*personal communication, we place two such circuits in mutual relation (but strip them of the body-codes which map and control the private internal environment) (figure 33).

The figures below show multiple values for each term. Thus P stands for all modes of perception, from *Gestalt*-perception in ordinary 'seeings' to religious emotions in the context of a theological system; R represents the corresponding responses, similarly ranging from common-sensical behavior patterns to activities based on reason, feeling and faith; C is the sum of the 'codes' in a given cultural person, whereby he couples input and output—perception and response; and E signals the particular environment, i.e. the Environment as it enters, analogously but not identically, into the experience of sender and receiver.

(33)

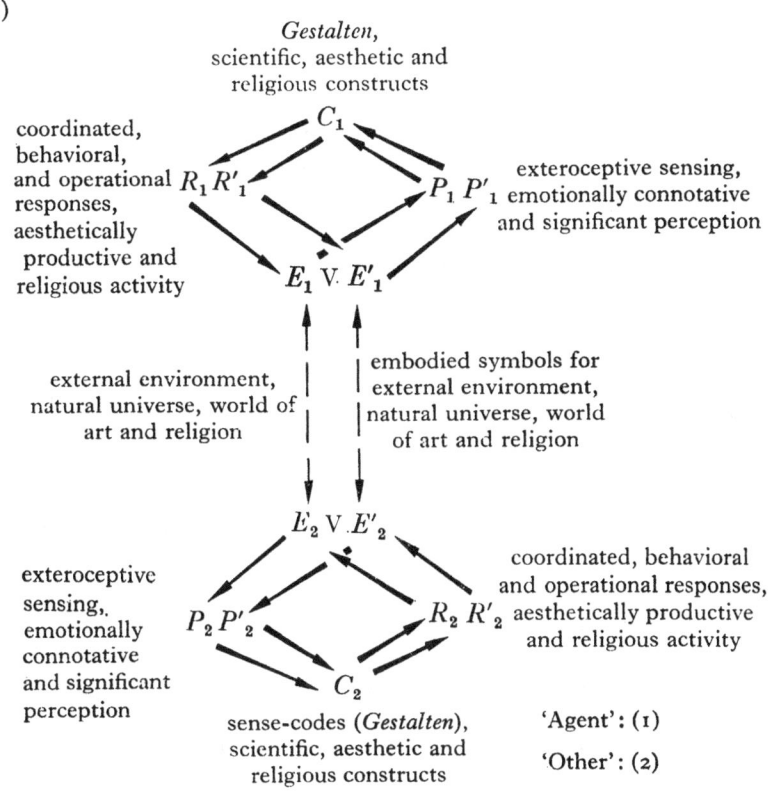

Interpersonal Communication:
general information-flow

A separate circuit of information-flow is marked in reference to the symbolized components of the environment, E'. The particular environment of the agent as well as of the Other gives rise either to perceptions which *exhibit* the characteristics in virtue of which they can be referred to the codes entertained by them; or to perceptions which *represent* these characteristics; or to both (E V E'). I may be walking in a forest, or hear you utter the word 'forest' or do both. These perceptions, traced to objectively different events in the Environment, differ among themselves and achieve a coincidence of meaning only by means of linguistic (or other) convention. The exhibiting as well as the representing perceptions conform to a common code, which may be a sensory *Gestalt* (such as trees and shrubs making up the *Gestalt* 'forest'), a scientific, aesthetic or religious construct, or a combination of them. But, notwithstanding the fact that the symbols and the events symbolized are mapped by common codes, the responses correlated with the perceptions differ. For example, although I mean the same by the word 'forest' as by the observation of trees and shrubs, I do not attempt to walk through the former, nor to write down the latter. Hence the common C's give rise to differentiated R's in commonly coded, but otherwise discrete circuits of symbolized and non-symbolized information-flow: $(P \cdot P') \rightarrow C \rightarrow (R \cdot R') \ldots$

The manipulative self-stabilization of the circuits of both sender and receiver are greatly facilitated by the technique introduced through the use of symbols. We know, on the basis of our previous considerations, that manipulative self-stabilization consists in the projection of our intrinsic codes into our environment, so that our resulting perceptions correspond to our actual knowledge. Symbols facilitate this process. Highways can be built, both literally and metaphorically, in reference to symbols. They are also traveled in reference to them. We can create and propagate scientific entities, artistic works, religious objects and the myriad gadgets and necessities which make up our produce, in reference to symbols. Some persons, such as scholars and accountants, spend the greater part of their day manipulating symbols, rather than the things symbolized.

Manipulative self-stabilization produces in our respective environment objects and events which correspond to our conceptions. But the respective environments of the agent and the Other are components in the encompassing Environment of both. Hence the respective manipulations of each has effect on the manipulation of the other. The relevant information chart is given in figure (34).

An event in the Environment (of which the particular environments of sender and receiver are localized perspectives) may be exhibiting or representing the characteristics in virtue of which its perceptions are referred to codes (i.e. such an event can be a symbol or an 'ordinary' object). The event (E or E') gives rise to analogous perceptions in persons equipped with similar sense organs (P_1 or P'_1 and P_2 and P'_2). If such persons further share a common body of knowledge in respect to their perceptions, their respective P's will be analogously referred (C_1 and C_2). Hence their responses will be likewise similar (assuming that C is the input-output coupling code), and thus their environmental manipulations (code projections) will coincide. As a result common types of symbolized and non-symbolized objects and events emerge in the Environment shared by the agent and the Other.

(34)

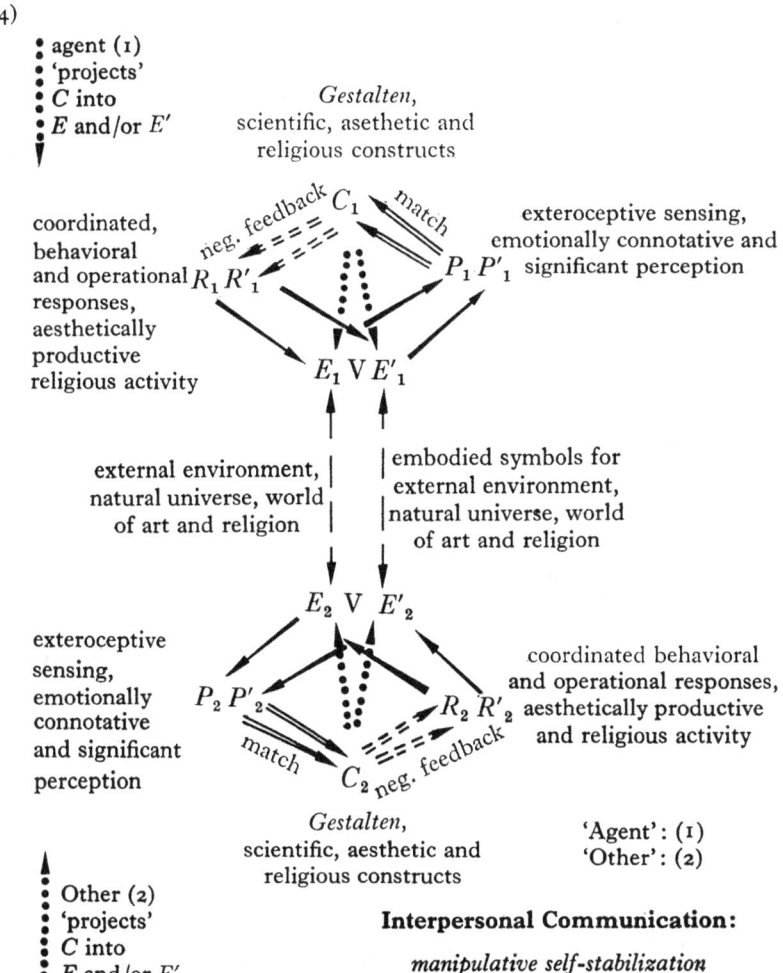

- agent (1)
- 'projects'
- C into
- E and/or E'

Gestalten, scientific, aesthetic and religious constructs

- Other (2)
- 'projects'
- C into
- E and/or E'

Gestalten, scientific, aesthetic and religious constructs

'Agent': (1)
'Other': (2)

Interpersonal Communication:

manipulative self-stabilization

The inclusion of symbols in the order imposed on the Environment facilitates communication, always provided that identically projected symbols are also identically mapped. Communication may not even make reference to the events which constitute the 'real' meaning of the symbols. Sets of symbols may be evolved, and through projection and mapping communicated, which make no reference to non-symbolized 'real' events. Such is the case in the axiomatic disciplines of logic and mathematics. Regardless of whether the symbols acquire autonomy, or are treated as convenient shorthand notation for the real environmental states which constitute their meaning, the projection of symbols by the agent yields significant perceptions for the Other, permitting the latter to map hitherto uncomprehended phenomena into his own codes, or lets him confirm his own codes by means of providing the relevant environmental exemplifications. In the latter sense persons with analogous cultural codes can, in manipulatively confirming their own codes in the environment, significantly contribute to the similar code-confirming activities of one another. Such activities put at our disposal 'ready-made' universes, including the "effective environments' of common sense, science, art and religion.

(35)

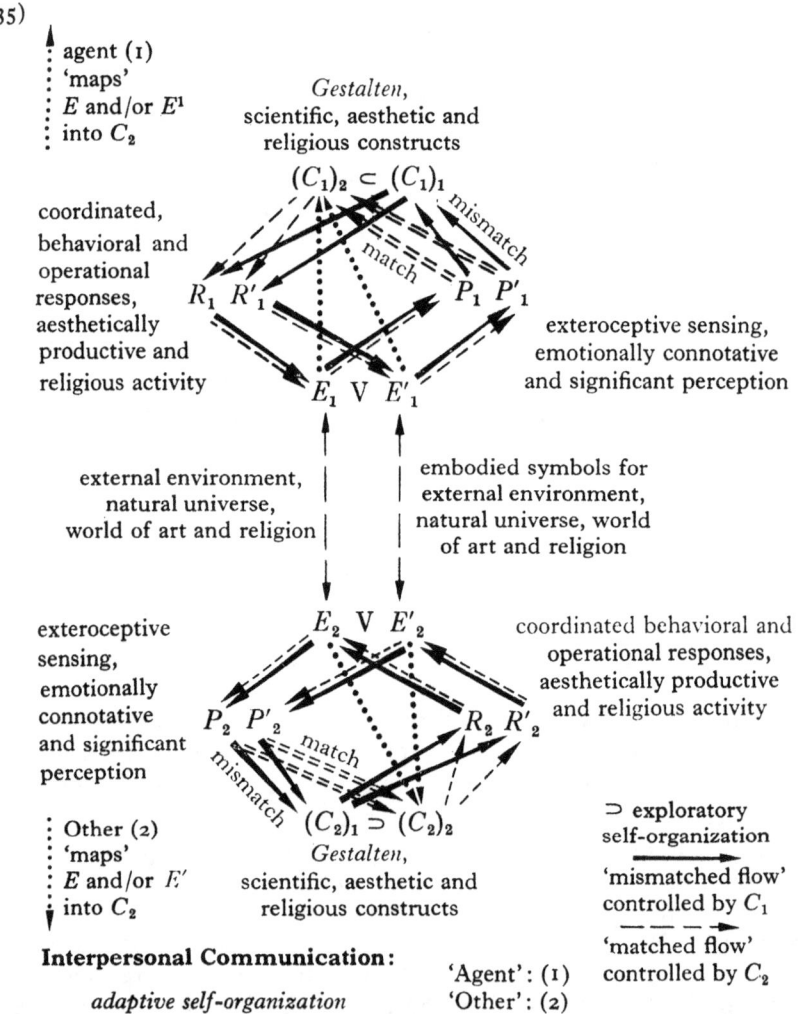

Interpersonal Communication:

adaptive self-organization

Self-*organization*, in other words 'learning' in the inclusive sense, is one more phenomenon we must take into consideration when dealing with interpersonal communication. There is a sense in which each of us is what he is in virtue of his Environment, and that Environment includes other persons, from whom we may learn. The emphasis on this aspect of the cognitive self-formative processes was emphasized by Whitehead when he said that 'the character of an actual entity is finally governed by its datum.' More specifically, his proposition is that 'It follows from this doctrine that the character of an organism depends on that of its environment.'[1] The problem is to show how the character of our self-stabilizing cognitive processes is organized in reference to the data provided by other cognizant human beings, making up part of our Environment. It can be elucidated by restating the interpersonal communications scheme in terms of adaptive self-organization (figure 35).

The general doctrine of adaptive self-organization is familiar from previous chapters. The environment is perceived, and the perception is referred to the codes and constructs available to the percipient. If the relation of the P's and the C is characterized by a 'mismatch signal' a problem is presented: the percepts cannot be accomodated as particular transformations of an invariant concept. Positive feedback activates free-running activities, exploring the degrees of freedom (intellectual-cultural capacities) of the system, leading to the envisagement of new C's. If the circuit of perception and response occurs in the framework of a 'match signal' (i.e. if the new C functions as the invariant element of the problematic P's), it is negative feedback stabilized and functions as the conceptual representation of E. The P's in question can be those which *exhibit* the characteristics in virtue of which they can be assimilated to the invariant C's, or they may be such as merely *represent* those characteristics because of an established convention. That is, it is immaterial from the viewpoint of adaptive self-organization whether the perceived environmental events are symbols or 'originals,' as long as it is known how the symbols are to be mapped (i.e. what their meaning is). Now, the specific contribution of interpersonal communication to the adaptive self-organization process is that it places at the receiver's disposal environmental events, symbolized as well as non-symbolized, which can be mapped by invariant codes and constructs. Adaptive self-organization is effectively facilitated if his perceptions include events which he does not as yet know, but which are the outcome of cognitive manipulation by the sender; that is, if the subject is made to perceive a problem which has been solved by someone else. The environmental events constituting the receiver's problem are then the embodiments

[1] Whitehead, *Process and Reality, op. cit.*, p. 168.

of the codes or constructs projected by the sender, presented to the receiver's perception in virtue of their sharing a common Environment. In ordinary langugage, learning is facilitated by presenting items of knowledge to the pupil, in the form of things, words, or writings, which embody the ideas. In that event the self-stabilizing manipulation of the environment of the teacher, whereby he structures his environment to correspond to his knowledge, issues in a set of ordered relations in the environment of his pupil, which the latter is encouraged to refer to his hypothesized knowledge. The communication of knowledge occurs necessarily by such means, since it is alone the Environment which is common to the experience of two persons, and thus that Environment must be ordered to things and symbols which embody the relevant knowledge. Failing the direct inspection of the sender's mind, such are the only means whereby the receiver could reconstitute in his own mind the knowledge present in that of the sender.

Learning in exclusive reference to theoretic meanings is one, but a relatively unusual case. Even then, it tends to be propaedeutic to applied knowledge. And in all cases, learning requires testing by means of trial and error activities within one's own circuit of coded activity. Thus, on the whole, knowledge is had by participation with the known. The participation renders the knowledge beneficial to all others sharing the Environment, since the knowledge of one, embodied in manipulatively projected environmental events (or symbols) may enter into their environment. Hence operationally tested knowledge adds to the Environment things to be known by the Other: it contributes to the datum of his experience and enriches it with further elements of potential meaning.

CHAPTER 5

Values in Cognitive Communication

The important, and today highly controversial question of values can be elucidated in the context of the foregoing analyses of the processes of cognition and communication.

Assume first that each person is a feedback-controlled cognitive system, directed toward the extraction of information from his environment. On the basic biological level the amounts of information thus extracted are necessary for the sustenance of life, information being, as Wiener has shown, 'the negative of a quantity usually defined as entropy in similar situations.'[1] On higher levels the information extracted from the environment is in the form of invariances discovered in the stream of experience and goes into the construction of effective environments, by means of which the cognizant being orients himself in his ambient. The cultural person is information-directed on multiple levels, and requires invariances in his experience in many respects, including the normalcy of his bodily (quasi-stationary) states, the intelligibility of his perceptions, the rationality, the aesthetic harmony and the transcendental significance of the world that surrounds him. The discovery of these invariances, and thereby the attainment of the corresponding informations, is the goal of the feedback-controlled transacting system which defines the vital activities of the human being. When an individual attains these goals, his directedness is fulfilled. It follows then that the discovery of invariant orders connotes *value* for the individual. (Whether in a given case the value is also social or merely individual, short or long term, depends on whether the discovered order *coincides* or *conflicts* with the information-extraction activities of others, and of the individual in the future.)

Value (in the above sense) can be communicated to an individual by another person by embodying in their commonly experienced Environment the types of order which, when perceived, can be assimilated to invariant codes or constructs by the former. If so, the embodied items represent information for the receiver, on any one of the many levels on

[1] Norbert Wiener, *Cybernetics*, New York, 1948. Negative entropy is the thermodynamic term for the element of order which the organism extracts from its environment. Cf. the Appendix, below.

94 *System, Structure, and Experience*

which he operates. Whether or not this is the case depends on the similarity of the code and construct systems of the communicators. If, for the sake of simplicity, we assume that the cognitive systems of sender and receiver are identical in all respects except one, and that the one respect in (36)

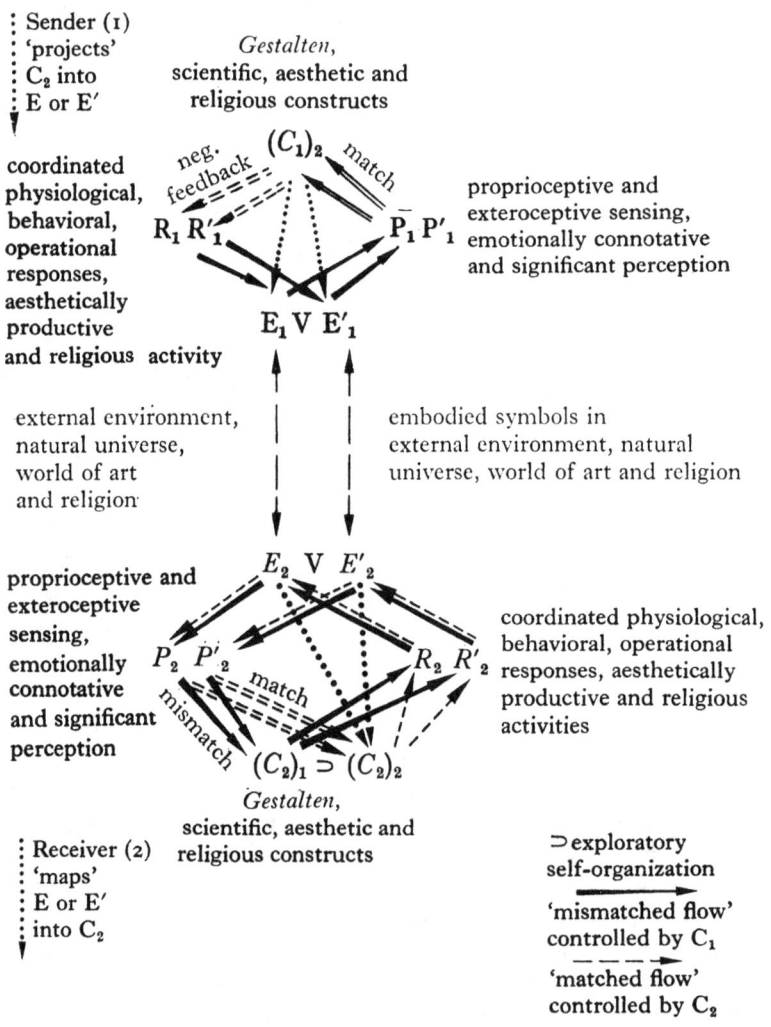

The Communication of Information (value)

which they are dissimilar is an extra 'bit' of information in the sender's system then the sender can communicate that extra item to the receiver by embodying in their commonly experienced Environment the type of order which either exhibits, or represents the information. Given the similarity of their cognitive systems in other respects, it is probable that the receiver will assimilate the order introduced into his experience by the sender to his existing *Gestalt* and construct systems. He will interpret the new experience similarly to the interpretation of the sender: he will *learn* from him. This process is represented in the information-flow chart of figure (36).

The graph depicts the scheme whereby a given *Gestalt* or construct (C_2) is communicated from sender to receiver. The sender operates in the manipulative, and the receiver in the adaptive mode. The information connoted by C_2 is of value to the receiver if it completes or improves his existing cognitive systems in some respect whereby they become more analytic or predictive of states in the environment, i.e. if through C_2 a further aspect of the environment can be mapped by his codes and constructs. In that event, C_2 represents value for the receiver, and the above graph depicts not merely the communication of information but that of value.

However, it now becomes clear that not every item which is of value to the sender is of value to the receiver. This depends on the existing cognitive systems of the latter. Value is relative to the existing *Gestalt* and construct frameworks. The deepest insight, if communicated to an infant or an idiot, is of less value to him than pointing at a furry household pet and saying 'cat.' Here, of course, 'value' is defined in reference to the cognitive goals of the individual and is identical with his personal satisfaction. (I am in accord on this point with Whitehead, for whom 'satisfaction' is the realization of the intrinsic 'subjective aim' of each entity. Cf. *Process and Reality*, pp. 29 ff.)

Now, *optimum* value is connoted by a pattern of activity which contributes to the development of the *Gestalt* and construct systems of the receiver either maximally on any one level, or on a maximum number of levels. Examples of the former include the feeding of infants, specialized education later in life, while examples of the latter comprise general child-raising as well as the over-all education needed to develop a well-rounded personality. I assume here that the higher intellectual cognitions not only do not exclude the satisfaction of more basic needs but presuppose them. In this view informations leading to satisfactions are built 'from the ground up': first the basic *Gestalten* of an intelligible perceptual world are helped to evolve, then those non-perceivable constructs are manipulatively added which permit the receiver to construct satisfactory scientific, aesthetic and religious universes for himself. Providing one of the latter prior to the former is putting the cart before the horse; as common sayings have it, one can neither study the nature of the universe nor appreciate the beauties of art while confused and hungry. (Compare Aristotle's views that friends, sufficient good looks, and practical experience are necessary before one can engage in living the 'contemplative life.')

The problem of value in communication presupposes the analysis of two basic factors. (*a*) the general types of objects and events which enter into human cognitive systems and thus have the potential of contributing to satisfaction; and (*b*) the particular types of cognitive systems of receivers. The here presented considerations intended to contribute to (*a*). Task (*b*) is a concrete and specific one, and cannot be theoretically generalized. But it is important to note that it presupposes (*a*): one cannot know what is likely to be relevant information to a person unless he also knows what types of informations are relevant to persons in general. Here the two factors in value communication correspond to the more general conceptions of *theory* and *practice*. Theory without practice is sterile, and practice without theory is blind. In value communication we need both the kind of theory I tried to present here, and the kind of application which can only be effected after a careful study of the particular constellation of ideas and beliefs of the person one is dealing with. If both factors are sufficiently taken into account, the sender can optimize the satisfaction of the receiver by embodying in their commonly experienced environments those events and symbols which complete and perfect the cognitive systems of the latter. Thus communication can be instrumental in building the optimally satisfying patterns of experience for people and, if having such experience is the intrinsic goal of human (as to a lesser extent of *all* living) beings, than communication has supreme value potential.

Theories of value are not proposed in a vacuum, but must find their place among the spectrum of ethical positions currently held. I should thus end these considerations by noting that great differences exist between the theory of value sketched above, and the general orientation of ethical theory in the anglo-saxon world. Analytical philosophers in this world predominate the field of ethics, and most of them center their attention on meta-ethics. Now, meta-ethics concentrates on the *sentences* stating value judgments and operates on the assumption that such sentences, if they are significant, must correspond to, or describe something. Thus the meta-ethical viewpoint of analysts (non-naturalist and non-cognitivists) is (*a*) linguistic, and (*b*) spectatorial. My own views differ from this in centering on the *situation* in which value-judgments are elicited, and in treating the judgments not as descriptive of, or corresponding to, something perceived in that situation, but as an outcome of the *structure* of the situation, elucidated as a systematic relationship between the experient and his surroundings. Consequently my own viewpoint is (*a*) contextual, more specifically system-theoretical, and (*b*) participatory, as opposed to spectatorial. I propose not a linguistic analysis of value sentences but a model of a system certain states of which represent its intrinsic goals and thus may, given that the system is an intelligent being, be verbalized as value pronouncements. Whether such uttered value judgments refer to anything empirical in the field of perception of the evaluator himself is immaterial for my analysis. Deciding this question depends in large measure on the cognitive value of subjective sensations, such as the satisfactions accompanying the discovery of an invariance in one's experience. But regardless of this question, values are assigned in my view to certain states of a system of transactions relating the agent to his environment, and are not limited to descriptive statements corresponding to something perceived by that agent. This, then, is the principal value-theoretical difference in standpoint between the theory presented here and the main thrust of contemporary meta-ethics. But if I have given the impression that my view stands alone today I should correct it: an increasing number of thinkers espouse something like my viewpoint, coming both from outside the analytical school (e.g. C. S. Pepper, Brand Blanshard, and Lancelot Law Whyte[1]), and from within it, voicing dissatisfactions with it (Stuart Hampshire, W. K. Frankena, and others[2]). Perhaps we shall witness, in the next decade or two, a reawakening of interest in moral theory as opposed to linguistic-analytical meta-ethics, and an orientation of such theory toward a transactional system-framework, so successfully used today by such fields as biology, ecology, cybernetics, management theory and communication theory.

[1] C. S. Pepper, *Concept and Quality*, LaSalle, Ill. 1966; Brand Blanshard, 'The New Subjectivism in Ethics' *Philosophy and Phenomenological Research*, IX (1949); Lancelot Law Whyte, 'Recover Values in a New Synthesis' in *Human Values and Natural Science*, ed. E. Laszlo and J. B. Wilbur, New York, 1970 (in the present series). I quote a passage from the last named study: 'to man, a coordinated organism with an ordering brain, order necessarily possesses value ... It is actually an expression of man's deepest nature, both as organism and as member of the species *homo sapiens*, to value order.'

[2] Stuart Hampshire, 'Fallacies in Moral Philosophy' *Mind*, LVIII (1949); William K. Frankena, 'Moral Philosophy at Mid-Century' *The Philosophical Review*, LX (1951). Similar criticisms have been voiced by H. D. Aiken, A. C. Ewing, H. J. Paton and A. M. MacIver.

CHAPTER 6

Conclusions

If we wish to evolve a scientific approach to the phenomenon of mind, we must learn to map out, in a consistent, adequate and yet economical theory, the basic structure of cognitive activity. That structure can now, for the first time in the history of thought, be studied in reference to the controlled findings of experimental sciences. The 'truth' thus discovered is stranger than the 'fiction' of even the most speculative of metaphysicians. The human mind, a phenomenon manifested by the complex operations of the nervous system of man, is not an autonomous entity which relates, either actively or passively but externally, to the 'outside' environment. Rather, the mind of man is a product of a series of normative interactions between environment and nervous system. The interactions involve the input and output of 'information': substances and energies in diverse forms. Mental operations are performed in the framework of these transactions and are themselves elements of it. The mind does not intuit anything just because it is 'there' in the environment: it experiences only that which conditions its processes of transaction. It used to be thought that we get to know what we experience, but it now turns out that we get to experience mostly what we already know (in the extended sense of 'know' in which we can also speak of the knowledge of the body and not only of conscious knowledge).

The precondition of proper functioning for the nervous system is an interactive relationship with the environment that corresponds to the intrinsic requirements of the system. Complex feedback-controlled homeostatic processes regulate the system in relation to the environment, and manipulate the environment in relation to the system. Adaptation and manipulation are both motivated by the built-in directionality of the system toward normal transactions. Normalcy is achieved in this regard when the system's input matches the various codes proper to it. Responses can then be correlated to maintain or correct the input for changes both in the system and in the environment. The regulative functions extend over a series of hierarchically organized circuits, with each higher circuit completing the one below it in some essential respect and achieving nonreducibility and a measure of autonomy through its specific types of codes.

Conclusions 99

But all circuits share the common motivation for closure (the matching of input and codes) and the higher circuits have relatively distinct manipulative and adaptive activities associated with them. Manipulation suits the environment to the codes, and adaptation adapts the codes to the environment. Self-stabilizing and self-organizing systems *project* their codes into states of their environment as well as *map* their environmental states into their codes. Such systems may equally well be artificial, biological or psychological.

Breathtaking perspectives open for the investigator interested in pursuing such considerations. He can gain an integrated and consistent view of diverse phenomena, referring them to isomorphically structured control systems. He can conceive of the unity of nature to lie in the realization of such systems in different forms and in different degrees of complexity and accomplishment. He can further consider that reality, long the elusive object of philosophical thought, may at last be grasped in terms of invariant systems. It may be that reality, as Margenau suggests, is associated with invariance. Then, the reality of mind, as well as the reality of the body, lies in the invariant information-flow control-systems which they represent. Likewise the reality of society, over and above the reality of its individual members, resides in the self-stabilizing and self-organizing social structure typical of all known forms of social organization. Such systems were thought, until relatively recently, to be unique to living things. At present, thanks to the pioneering work of cyberneticians, information theorists, general system theorists, system-analysts, structural anthropologists, structural linguists, and their fellow workers in related fields, we come to the insight that the properties of the systems are independent of the origin, material and individual identity of their components. The same regulatory system, expressed in an information-flow chart, may be realized as an artificial system composed of transistors and capacitors, as a hydrodynamic or mechanical system, and as a system of nervous pathways and synapses. The exploratory hypotheses of this work suggest that, underlying the complex phenomena of the human mind, and of human interrelations formed by communicating human beings, there is a basic regulatory structure which is shared by the biological body and by artificial servomechanisms. The degrees of accomplishment (in Wiener's term, the 'orders of prediction and extrapolation') may differ, and the materials and their mode of interconnection can be diverse. But the integrated logic of the functional information-flows can be isomorphic, and in that isomorphism we may recognize the fundamental unity of nature, expressed in heterogeneous forms.

The vistas are wide, the perspectives enticing. Specialization, which has brought us detailed analytic understanding of specific phenomena, may be balanced by general theories, not relinquishing precision but integrating the detailed findings in balanced frameworks whereby the true meaning of the isolated facts brought forth by special analyses may become evident. The systematization of knowledge, as Whitehead noted, cannot be conducted in watertight compartments, for all general truths condition one another.[1] One such systematization has been attempted here, by adopting the concepts and techniques of modern systems research. It has not reached more than a fraction of the territory open for such treatment and has not done more than offer reasoned hypotheses. But by so doing it may have demonstrated the feasibility and the rewards of pressing forward and have encouraged further research into this promising new field of inquiry. It may be that the theory of mind, as the domain which studies the many varieties of human experience, is entering into a period of transition from speculative philosophy to empirical science. If so, sustained research into its problems, traditionally dealt with by philosophy, can be both challenging and fruitful if undertaken in the context of modern systems theory.

---

[1] *Process and Reality, op. cit.,* p. 15.

APPENDIX

Further Notes on the Perception of Invariant Intelligible *Gestalten*

As noted in Chapter 3 (pp. 43ff), one of the outstanding and most puzzling facts of sensory experience is the perception of invariant and intelligible *Gestalten* on the basis of a constantly varying stream of sensory stimulation. We appear to 'see' certain localizations of invariant universals, rather than what meets our eye. The controversy centered on this question in philosophy was a lengthy and, on the whole, an unprofitable one. My purpose in these additional notes is not to review it, but to (i) argue that we do indeed see more than meets our eyeball, and (ii) explore some hypothetical solutions as to the remarkable processes whereby we may do so.

Consider the assertion, 'we see localized universals, not sense-perceived particulars.' This is not to doubt that the raw material of our perceptions is made up of particular 'data,' but only to contest that when we say 'this is x' we mean nothing more than collections of such data. I contend that we mean localized universals, i.e. invariant intelligible *Gestalten*, clothed in the materials of sense-data.

A striking case can be made for this assertion in reference to a 'sense-object' known to all parents most intimately and, as it would seem, immediately: 'our child.' Surely, most parents will contend, we know our child; not our *Gestalt* 'child.' Yet common-sensical parents have to be disappointed. We know our child by his figure, the set of his mouth, the way his hair falls, his mode of speech, his pattern of behavior and a thousand other characteristics. Jointly these identify our child even among a million others. But does this mean that we identify our child because we are familiar with our direct perceptions of him, or because we established a set of universal codes in regard to him? Whether we like it or not, we must affirm the latter. We know our child not by our direct perceptions of him, for each of these is unique and perishing, but by the combination of many characteristics which we abstracted from our past perceptions and established in our mind as our *Gestalt* 'child.' It is because we can draw upon a large number of such characteristics, uniquely combined in our *Gestalt* that we can pick out our child among many others. When our 'localization of universals' is poorer, our powers of identification likewise diminish. A yellow marble in a bag of marbles containing dozens of such coloring is not identifiable again if lost from sight. Our *Gestalt* 'yellow marble' fits all such marbles without distinction. But if we add a further 'universal' to one marble, e.g. in the form of a scratch mark, we can pick it out from among all unscratched marbles. But then we would not have a better claim for having known that particular marble in itself: we could only claim to have had a more distinctive *Gestalt* of it. And thus even with our child: we know him so precisely because we have an extraordinarily distinctive *Gestalt* of him. It is thus our *Gestalt* that we know, clothed in the sensuous material of our momentary perceptions. Ironically but truthfully we can say that we recognize *any* series of perceptions as our child provided that it shares the characteristic combination of universals which constitute our *Gestalt*. If any series of perceptions fails to correspond to our *Gestalt* we refuse to identify it as our child, even though it may well be of our child. Such is the case when, after a long period of absence, we confront a grown son and fail to recognize him. Recognition comes when there is independent reason to believe that he is in fact our son (he identifies himself, or others do so) and we can relate our previous child-*Gestalt* to the *Gestalt* of the grown man before us. Cognition, as I said, presupposes recognition, and recognition is in terms of C's, not P's. 'Seeing,' Hanson points out, 'is a "theory-laden" understanding. Observation of x is shaped by prior knowledge of x.' He queries, 'How should we regard a man's report that he sees x if we know him to be ignorant of all x-ish things? Precisely as we would regard a four-year old's report that he sees a meson shower.'[1] Yet we do not ask, Hanson says, 'What's that' of every passing bicycle. Instead of merely seeing objects (presumably as they are in themselves) we see them *as* something—something previously experienced and therefore familiar—such as bicycles. We recognize familiar *Gestalten* to which the variety of our perceptions are reduced, or assimilated to, or, if you prefer, in terms of which they are interpreted. This is what I mean when I say that our P's are referred to C's and are known in terms of the latter.

But what if our P's *cannot* be referred to C's? If, due to some deficiency in the P-plane, none of our established sense-codes apply? If that is momentarily the case, we are temporarily puzzled. But when the situation persists, more serious consequences are entailed. Here I may refer again to the so-called 'sensory deprivation' experiments.

In such experiments the sensory input is significantly reduced. Volunteers may be placed in isolation chambers with their hands and heads

[1] N. R. Hanson, *op. cit.*, Chapter 1, p. 21.

wrapped in bandages, or floated in warm pools, touching nothing, hearing but a low hum, seeing only a dim light. The subjects, who entered the experiments without particular misgivings, came close to breaking down after a relatively short lapse of time. They lost their sense of time, their remembrance of things and their ability to concentrate; they had hallucinations. In some cases they had to be pulled out after a few hours, in others they endured the experiment for some days. Then they emerged staggering, unable to answer simple questions, and categorically refusing to repeat the experiment. For days their perception and problem-solving ability were below normal. One physiologist concluded that 'our brains organize, and exist to organize, a great variety of incoming sensory messages every waking second, and can become not only emotionally upset but seriously deranged if these messages cease or even if they cease to be new.' The mind's need for richly structured experiential input, he points out, is present in adults as well as infants and is present all through our lives.[1]

A non-varied stream of P's is not only an enigma for the mind; it is a pathological disturbance. Varied P's are the precondition both of sensory cognition and of normal mental functioning. In its normal operation, our mind performs the remarkable feat of spontaneously organizing varied and fluctuating P's into invariant and familiar C's. How is this feat possible? The field of neurophysiology is not yet advanced enough to give a definitive answer but, now that I touched upon physiological evidence, I should point out the possibility that such answer may one day be forthcoming. This expectation is based on the brilliant, though highly speculative, work of McCulloch and Pitts. They affirmed the distinct possibility, that this operation is indeed performed by our higher nervous system.

McCulloch and Pitts proposed two neural mechanisms which would exhibit the properties necessary for the 'recognition of invariant forms' (or 'universals') in reference to variable sensory stimuli. They have 'focussed attention on particular mechanisms in order to reach explicit notions about them which guide both histological studies and experiment.' And, they point out, 'if mistaken, these notions still present the possible kinds of hypothetical mechanisms and the general character of circuits which recognize universals, and give practical methods for their design.'[2]

By the 'recognition of universals' the authors mean the visual and auditory perception of invariant forms, in reference to complex neural nets embodied in the nervous structure. In vision, the 'perception of universals'

[1] John R. Platt, 'The Fifth Need of Man,' *Horizon*, July 1959.
[2] Walter Pitts and Warren S. McCulloch, 'How We Know Universals: The Perception of Auditory and Visual Forms,' *Bulletin of Mathematical Biophysics*, 1947, Vol. 9.

is the ability of the nervous system to 'detect the equivalence of apparitions related by similarity and congruence, like those of a single physical thing seen from various places.' The analogous perception in hearing is signified by the recognition of timbre and chord, regardless of pitch. As McCulloch and Pitts note, these equivalent apparitions share a common figure and define a group of transformations which take the equivalents into one another while preserving the figure invariant. For example, 'a group of translations' removes a visual square appearing at one place to other places, yet it leaves the *figure* of the square invariant. These figures, the authors suggest, are the 'geometric objects' of Cartan and Weyl and the '*Gestalten*' of Köhler and Wertheimer. Evidently, they are also the universals of Plato and Aristole, given a physiologically conceptualist interpretation.

McCulloch and Pitts seek to outline a design for nervous nets which could account for such universals, geometrical objects, and *Gestalten*. They conceive the problem as the finding of nets 'which recognize figures in such a way as to produce the same output for every input belonging to the [given] figure.'

Two mechanisms are suggested. The first mechanism averages a visual or auditory apparition over a group; the second reduces an apparition to a standard selected from among its many previous presentations.

The former mechanism resolves the problem, how a finite group of transformations can carry such functions which describe apparitions into their equivalents of the same (invariant) figure. If G is the finite group of transformations and T is its transformation, then four problems of ascending complexity can be distinguished: (i) T's of G are linear and generated by transformations of the underlying manifold; (ii) T's of G are linear but cannot be so generated; (iii) T's of G are linear but depend also upon the time factor (e.g. upon a moving average over preceding synaptic delays in the firing of the neurons in the nets); and (iv) not all T's of G are linear.

Solutions to these problems are sought in nervous nets which include 'time-scanning.' This device illustrates the principle called the 'exchangeability of time and space.' 'This states that any dimension or degree of freedom of a manifold or group can be exchanged freely with as much delay in the operation as corresponds to the number of distinct places along that dimension.' Histological data are presented to support the thesis that nervous nets exist wherein the interchanging of spatial and temporal processes could conceivably take place (e.g. in Heschl's gyrus [a strip of cortex on the superior surface of the temporal lobe] and in the 'granular layer' of Brodmann). Neural nets in these areas are postulated, which might perform the auditory, respectively the visual, perception of universals through time-scanning. For example, the proposed auditory mechanism is described as follows. 'Impulses of some chord enter slantwise along the specific afferents... and ascend until they reach the [given] level... in the columns of the receptive layer activated at the moment by the nonspecific afferents. These provide summation adequate to permit the impulses to enter that level but no other. From there the impulses descend along columns to the depth. The level in the column, facilitated by the nonspecific afferents, moves repetitively up and down, so that the excitement delivered to the depth moves uniformly back and forth as if the sounds moved up and down together in pitch, preserving intervals. In the deep columns various combinations are made of the excitation and are averaged during a cycle of scansion to produce results depending only on the chord.' Hence an auditory form—in this case the chord—would be perceived as invariant, regardless of changes in the pitch. An analogous mechanism would scan invariant visual forms by interchanging spatial dimension and time through specific delays in the operation.

The visual mechanism proposed by McCulloch and Pitts reduces a series of sensory impressions of a given type to a preselected standard. The nervous nets proposed to perform this function are referred to as 'reflex-mechanisms': they operate on the principle of negative feedback. It is argued that if e.g. a square should appear anywhere in the visual field, the eyes turn until it is centered, and what they perceive is the same, regardless of the initial position of the square. The performance of this mechanism is clarified by the following formalization. Out of a series of transforms T of a sensory apparition, one of them, e.g. ϕ is chosen as the standard. When presented with ϕ, the mechanism computes one or more suitable parameters $a(\phi)$, $b(\phi)$, ..., which uniquely define its position within the transforms $T\phi$ so that their simultaneous equality, $a(\phi) = a(s\phi)$, $b(\phi) = b(s\phi)$, etc., is sufficient to entail the relation of identity, $S = I$. If there are persistent errors, a suitable mechanism eliminates them. For example, the persistent errors $E_1(\phi) = a(\phi) - a(\phi_0)_1$ $E_2(\phi) = b(\phi) - b(\phi_0)_1$ impel the mechanism to perform the operation $T\phi$ so determined as to diminish the parameters $E(T\phi)$ as compared to $E(\phi)$. The operation may be repeated until the $E(\phi)$'s vanish (through their progressive reduction with each repetition) and $\phi = \phi_a$; i.e. *invariance to a standard is secured*. The mechanism is circular, with some of the output being fed back to activate the computation of error. Hence the output is highly determined by the neural nets, and is not a direct consequence of the input.

Northrop has assessed the epistemological significance of such neural nets. In this words, 'Newton, among others, pointed out that the structure of sensed space and time is relative to the particular observer and quite different from the structure of public, mathematical space and time to which the theories of experimentally verified physics refer. Einstein continues this Newtonian distinction. An adequate, neurologically grounded theory of knowledge must account, therefore, for the manner in which the knower distinguishes the public, indirectly verified, postulationally designated structures and entities of natural science from the immediately sensed ones. This entails an account of how the nervous system, which receives impulses epistemologically correlated with images varying from moment to moment and standpoint to standpoint, arrives at invariant entities and relations holding constant through the changing, immediately apprehended particulars. McCulloch and Pitts have shown that such invariants can be achieved by complicated neural nets which scan and average over a group of transformations.'[1] Northrop concludes that traditional theories of mind rest upon an oversimplified notion of nervous activity: they assume that such activity is linear. It is entirely warranted, however, to assume that the firing sequence of neurons in the nervous system is predominantly circular. Northrop then considers the simplest possible case of a noncircular ordering of neurons, the one in which an afferent neuron a is joined to another afferent or motor neuron, b. Assume that the firing of neuron a is the signal which entails the firing of neuron b as the behavioristic response. Then, if no further action occurs with respect to a, the signal which is its firing perishes; the firing of b is a response which does not affect a. Regardless of how many neurons are ordered into such a noncircular sequence, the firing of any neuron in the nervous system could only signify what happened at the corresponding instant, and such higher nervous activities as memory, abstract thought (including the knowing of universals), the entertainment of purpose, etc., could not be accounted for. Now suppose that a finite set of neurons are ordered in a *circular* sequence. The signal which is the firing of a fires b, this in turn fires c . . ., until the signal is eventually returned to a, by the last neuron (other than a) giving a signal which results in the firing of a. Then, assuming that the time it takes the impulses to succeed one another around the circuit is sufficient to permit the neurons to restore their energies between firings from the metabolic activities of the organism, the signals represented by the firing of the neurons will not perish but may continue indefinitely. Points of entry into such regenerative, or 'reverberating' loops (also described by Lorente de No) are provided by afferent neurons located in the sense organs. Output is through the neurons transmitting muscular innervations

[1] F. S. C. Northrop, 'The Neurological and Behavioristic Psychological Basis of the Ordering of Society by Means of Ideas,' *Science*, Vol. 107, No. 2782.

and other impulses to motor centers in the various parts of the organism. Since the regenerative loop 'preserves the form of the fact without reference to the one particular moment when it was experienced,' and averages over, as well as reduces to a preselected standard, the signals fed into it, it enables the response to occur to an invariant 'form' rather than to the variable sensory input. The loops assimilate the variable elements transmitted from the sense organs to invariant *Gestalten*. Thus they effect an 'invariance to a standard' of the sensory input. In my terminology this means that variable P's are referred to invariant C's as the latter's transformations. If and when that happens, we cognize our perceptions in terms of our *Gestalten*: we see the shape *as* a bicycle, even if we have never seen one like this before, and even when the light changes. We recognize our child even if he wears a new suit and our house when its roof is covered with snow.

The precise neural processes which permit us to see things as invariant intelligible *Gestalten* are not known with certainty and it is not clear whether they can ever be thus known. But difficulties in observation and experimental confirmation can only prevent hypothetical principles from becoming reliable theoretical constructs, and not from being envisaged as logical necessities in the face of circumstantial evidence. The latter is the case here. Our minds *must* (there being no alternatives as far as I can see) be capable of reducing, or assimilating, their variable input to invariant universals by some neurological process, since we do know that our experience is made up of a fluctuating caleidoscopic stream whereas its contents are relatively stable, recurrent entities. The invariance-extraction process poses a primarily neurological problem on the sense-perceptual level, where we spontaneously *see* our data *as* intelligible *Gestalten*. The same process is encountered on the higher, 'cultural' circuits, where consciously elaborated theoretic, aesthetic and religious constructs take the place of the *Gestalten*. But the crucial issue of neurological coding and de-coding cannot be avoided, for even the higher invariance-extracting operations are performed by our nervous system, albeit in reference not to actually perceived 'seen' data, but in recourse to 'felt,' or conceptualized and symbolized, experiences. The information-flow design proposed in this work rests on the assumption of a passage from variable input to invariant codes and, although the neurological mechanism which would satisfy this postulate is not known, it assumes its existence. Hypotheses of the McCulloch, Pitts, de No and Northrop variety adduce evidence of the practical feasibility of such mechanisms in our nervous system. If the mechanisms would be morphologically discovered we would have a scientific theory of *brain*, as the locus of higher cognitive activity. But already if the *logic* of the mechanisms is elucidated, a scientific theory of *mind* can result. My own effort in this respect gains added significance in view of the fact that it conceptualizes the cognitive extension of the very process upon which life depends. Life, as Schrödinger said, depends on an organization which maintains itself by extracting order from the environment.[1] The invariance-extracting mechanism of perception, and the related invariance-extracting activities of science, art and religion, extend this basic life-process into the domain of 'philosophical' and 'psychological' phenomena. In the light of the present information-flow design, these phenomena can be likewise analyzed to the extraction of order from the environment. And in this perspective the perception of invariant *Gestalten* on the basis of a constantly fluctuating stream of stimulation is the essential link between the organism's negentropic order-extraction functions and the cultural mind's sophisticated scientific and aesthetic ordering processes.

---

[1] Erwin Schrödinger, *What Is Life?* Cambridge, 1962.

Index

Abstract operations 9
Activity, aesthetic 57–69
  cultural 46–77
  perceptual-cognitive 36–46
  physiological 29–36
  religious 69–75
  scientific 51–57
'Actual occasion (entity)' 21, 91
Adaptation 5, 9, 14, 15, 35, 45f, 49–50, 68–69, 74f, 77, 91, 98
Adversion 59–61
Aesthetics 57–69
AIKEN, H. D. 97n
AMES, A. 42
ARISTOTLE 43, 96, 104
Art, information-flow of 57–69
Artificial systems 7f, 15
Artist 66f
ASHBY, W. R. 12
Atom 20
Aversion 59–61

BARTOK, B. 67
BERKELEY, Bishop G. 17
BERNARD, C. 30
BERTALANFFY, L.v. 30
BEXTON, W. H. 47
Biological organism 12ff, 26
BLANSHARD, B. 97
Brain 21, 103, 107
BREGER, L. 45n
BRUNSWICK, E. 42
BULLOUGH, E. 65n

CANNON, W. B. 13n, 32, 51
CANTRIL, H. 42
CASSIRER, E. 65n, 66
Causal efficacy 40
Cell 20

Checker-playing learning machine 9–12
CHOPIN, F. 67
Closed system 12
Codes 2ff
  meta-sensory 50–77
  physiological 31–35
  sensory 36–46
Cognition, perceptual 38–46
Cognitive systems 94f
COLLINGWOOD, R. G. 58, 62, 64, 66
Communication, interpersonal 78–97
  intrapersonal 80–81, 86
Communication of information (value) 94–95
Confirmation (in science) 55–56
Construct 27
  aesthetic 59–69
  epistemically connected 53n
  formally connected 54n
  rational (scientific) 51–57
  religious 70–75
Control element (apparatus) 8f, 30f, 38
CROCE, B. 58–59, 64n, 66
Culture 47ff, 76–77
Cybernetics vii, 99

DESCARTES, R. 17
Directive correlation 6, 12, 13

EINSTEIN, A. 84
Emotion 59
Empirical-rationalist method 17f, 41, 55f
Empiricism 16f
  radical 17, 51
Environment 5ff, 23
  effective 24f, 27, 29, 32, 77, 82f

Epistemic correlation 40–41
Epistemological problem 39–41
Epistemology 16ff
Ethics 96–97
EWING, A. C. 97n
Experience viiff
  primitive 59, 61, 65
  objects and subjects of 20f
Expression (in art) 64f
Exteroception 36ff

Feedback stabilization 13–15, 26
Feeling 59, 61
'Feeling as' 59f
'Feeling that' 70–75
Focal condition 13
Form, platonic 43
FRANKENA, W. K. 97
Free-running activities 10, 91
FRY, R. 58, 65n, 66
Functionalist psychology of perception 42
Fundamentalism 75

General Adaptation Syndrome 33
General System Theory vii, 15, 99
Gestalt 38ff, 49, 52f, 78f, 101–108
Gestalt Psychology 42
Gestalt-system 39ff, 51, 57, 95
GIBSON, J. J. 42
Goal-directedness 3f, 8f
Goal of feedback 13, 33f
GRASTYÁN, E. 59–60

Hamlet 64
HAMPSHIRE, S. 97
HANSON, N. R. 44, 54–55, 64, 102
Healing 33
Health 35
HEBB, D. O. 48
HEGEL, G. W. F. 17
HERON, W. 47
Hierarchy of information-flow circuits 29, 46, 76–77
Homeostasis 13f, 28, 30, 32f, 46
Homeostat 12n
Homeostatic feedback circuit 29–36, 38, 46
Human body 10, 30–36

HUME, D. 17, 18, 41, 43, 51, 83
HUXLEY, J. 14
Hypothesis 10, 11, 45, 75, 98

Infant 37–38
Information-flow model of mind 2ff, 23, 29ff, 98
Information pool, genetic 35
Information theory vii, 99
Input 2ff
Input-norm correspondence 48f, 98
Intelligence 37–38, 77
Intelligibility, criterion of 3, 49
Internal environment (*milieu intérieur*) 24f, 30–35
Interpretation of experience vii, 16, 29
Introspection 22, 39–41
Invariance extracting system 2f, 93, 107–108
Isomorphy 8ff, 29, 47, 76, 99
ITTELSON, W. H. 42

JAMES, W. 69–71

KAHLER, E. 58
KANT, I. 17, 83
KARMOS, G. 60n
KELÉNYI, L. 60n
KILPATRICK, F. P. 42
KÖHLER, W. 104
KOFFKA, K. 42n

LASZLO, E. 41, 97n
Learning 10–12, 45f, 56, 91f
LEIBNITZ, G. W. 17
LENIN, V. I. 42
Levels of information-flow 29, 46–47, 50, 76–77, 78f
LILLIE, R. 27

MACIVER, A. M. 97n
MACKAY, D. M. 7–10
Macromolecule 20
Manipulation 6, 14, 15, 34, 44, 49–50, 65, 77, 85, 98
MARGENAU, H. 13n, 52n, 54n, 56, 70, 99
MARTIN, J. 60n
Matched-flow 3ff

Match-signal 8f
MCCULLOCH, W. 43, 103–106, 107
Meta-ethics 96
Meta-sensory feedback circuit 29, 46–77
MILNER, P. 60n
Mind 1, 2, 7, 98, 100, 108
Mind-body problem 1
Mismatched-flow 5ff
Mismatch-signal 8ff
Motivation 48f, 61
MURPHY, G. 42

Natural science 19f
Negative feedback 4f, 8f, 14f
Nervous system 14, 21, 23, 25, 31, 34, 47
Neural nets 104–107
Neuron 106
Neurophysiology 27, 42, 59–60, 104–107
No, L. de 106, 107
Norm of sensory stimulation 48
NORTHROP, F. S. C. 58, 105–107

Observation (in science) 52–56, 69
OLDS, J. 60
Open system 12
Operational response 53–56
Order in environment 85f, 93, 97
Output 2ff

PARKER, D. H. 65n
PARMENIDES 17
PATON, H. J. 97n
PEPPER, S. C. 40, 66, 97
Perception 23, 42f, 51, 88f, 101–108
PIAGET, J. 37
PITTS, W. 43, 103–106, 107
PLATO 17, 43, 104
PLATT, J. R. 103
Positive feedback 5f, 10f
Prägnanz, law of 42
Presentational immediacy 40
Proprioception 24, 31ff
Protocol 53
Psychology, experimental 42

Rationalism 16, 51f

READ, Sir H. 63–64
Reality 99
Receiver ('Other') 81–92, 94–96
Reductionism 26f, 39
Reflective consciousness 77
Reflex-arc 26
Relativity theory 83–84
Religion 69–75
Response, to art 65–67
    to perceptual cognition 44
    to religion 73–75
    to science 53–56
Reverberating loops 106–107
RUSSELL, Lord B. 52

Scale of evaluation 11
Scepticism 16f, 51
Schemata 37
SCHRÖDINGER, E. 108
Science, information-flow of 51–57
SCOTT, T. H. 47
'Seeing as' 43f, 80
'Seeing that' 54f, 80
Self-organization 5f, 9f, 14f, 24f, 35, 57, 74f, 91, 99
Self-stabilization 4f, 14f, 24f, 34f, 44f, 56, 65f, 73f, 76, 88f, 99
SELYE, H. 33
Sender ('agent') 81–92, 94–96
Sense of presence 70–73
Sensory deprivation 47, 102–103
Sensory feedback circuit 29, 36–46
Sign 85
SINNOTT, E. W. 27, 28, 34
SOMMERHOFF, G. 6, 12, 13
Space-time continuum 83
Stationary states 14, 32, 36
STRAUSS, R. 63
Stress 33f
Structuralism 1, 2, 28, 99
Stylistic change (in the arts) 68
Symbol 80–92
Symbolic reference 40
Systems-analysis *vii*, 1, 15
System-theory 1, 2, 15, 16, 28, 51, 100

THAYER, L. 81
Theology 70–75
Thermodynamics 18

THORNTON, R. W. 13
Time-scanning 104–105
Transactionalist psychology of perception 41f

Universals 101, 103–106
Universe of science 53–57, 84

Value 93–97
 judgment of 96–97
 optimum 95
 theories of 96–97

VERECZKEY, L. 60n
Verifact 56

WEITZ, M. 57–58
WERTHEIMER, M. 104
WEYL, 104
WHITEHEAD, A. N. *vii, viii*, 21, 22, 28, 40, 41, 43, 59, 60, 69, 70, 84, 91, 100
WHYTE, L. L. 97
WIENER, N. 6, 9, 10, 11, 13n, 93, 99

For Product Safety Concerns and Information please contact our EU
representative GPSR@taylorandfrancis.com
Taylor & Francis Verlag GmbH, Kaufingerstraße 24, 80331 München, Germany